ROGER JONES

trotman

Charity and Voluntary Work

UNCOVERED

Charity and Voluntary Work Uncovered

This first edition published in 2006 by Trotman and Company Ltd
2 The Green, Richmond, Surrey TW9 1PL

© Trotman and Company Limited 2006

Editorial and Publishing Team

Author Roger Jones
Editorial Mina Patria, Editorial Director; Jo Jacomb, Editorial
Manager; Catherine Travers, Managing Editor; Ian Turner,
Editorial Assistant
Production Ken Ruskin, Head of Manufacturing and Logistics;
James Rudge, Production Artworker
Advertising Tom Lee, Commercial Director

Designed by XAB

British Library Cataloguing in Publication Data
A catalogue record for this book is available from the British Library

ISBN 978 1 84455 103 3

Typeset by Mac Style, Nafferton, East Yorkshire
Printed and bound by Creative Print & Design Group, Wales

CONTENTS

About the Author

Roger Jones has worked in the charity and voluntary sector, both as a volunteer and a salaried staff member, and is currently a charity trustee. He has written a number of careers handbooks, including *You Want to Work Where?!* and *Real Life Guide: Electrician* (both published by Trotman), *Getting a Job Abroad* and *Getting a Job in America*.

Acknowledgements

A number of people and organisations have helped me with this book and I would particularly like to thank Rosie Dick, Martin Horwood, Ruth Mantle, Ian Parker, Nicola Schofield, Ros Wild and staff at the Directory for Social Change.

Roger Jones

INTRODUCTION

Have you ever done a sponsored walk for the British Heart Foundation? Or responded to a British Red Cross appeal to provide relief for a disaster on the other side of the world? Perhaps you have helped out in your local Age Concern shop? Or manned a stall at a charity fete? You may even have organised a special fundraising event for Children in Need?

These are just a few of the more visible activities of the voluntary sector in the UK. Most charities and voluntary organisations rely a lot on voluntary help, especially with the fundraising aspects. But while some rely entirely on such help, others employ staff to carry out some of the duties which are too onerous to be carried out in a person's spare time. It is on these salaried posts within a range of different organisation that this book will focus.

WHY READ THIS BOOK?

This book is aimed at two kinds of reader:

- A person who has not yet embarked on a career and wants to explore the different options available before taking the plunge

- A person who has work experience, but feels the time has come to try something different – a career change.

If you are planning a journey anywhere, it makes sense to find out as much as possible about where you are going before you leave. The same applies to finding a job. If you know what a particular job entails, you can make a considered judgement as to how well suited you are to a job and whether it meets your needs and aspirations.

While the salary on offer could have a bearing on your final decision, other factors are equally important. You also need to ask yourself the following questions:

● Would I find this kind of work interesting?

● Have I the right qualifications for it?

● Do I have the right experience and skills?

● Have I the right personality for this work?

● Would I feel at ease working in the voluntary sector?

This book aims to give you an insight into what working in the voluntary/charity sector is like. It will look at a wide range of charitable and voluntary organisations, but excludes housing associations, government controlled charities, independent schools (many of which have charitable status) and organisations whose primary purpose is the promotion of religion.

WHY CONSIDER A JOB IN THE VOLUNTARY SECTOR?

Many people imagine that working for a charitable or voluntary organisation means working for no salary. Of course, millions of people undertake unpaid voluntary work and this is much appreciated. However, many organisations, particularly the larger ones, do not rely on volunteers alone.

In fact, at the present time over 600,000 people work for voluntary organisations on a salaried basis: as fundraisers, organisers, administrators, etc. Altogether they account for 2.2% of Britain's workforce. This compares with over 20 million in the private sector and nearly 7 million in public sector jobs.

This may sound small, but the voluntary sector is expanding. The number of organisations has grown by 28,000 since 2000 and this expansion has created 45,000 new jobs. The current rate of job growth is around 10,000 per year. By contrast, the number of jobs in the private sector has fallen in recent years.

Achieving a healthy work–life balance is an important consideration for many people, and the voluntary sector scores highly with people who wish to work part-time. Nearly 40% of the workforce is employed on a part-time basis and opportunities for more flexible working arrangements seem to be growing yearly. This is of particular interest to women who account for around two-thirds of voluntary sector jobs.

Another important consideration is that on the whole voluntary sector workers have more job satisfaction than those in the public and private sectors according to a survey conducted by Warwick University. On a scale of one to seven the average scores were:

- Voluntary sector: 5.72

- Public sector: 5.45

- Private sector: 5.35.

Various reasons were given for the higher scores including:

- Undertaking work in tune with your values

- Seeing the results of the work you do

- Not being part of the rat race

- Encouragement and commitment.

Generally speaking, charities have a reputation for being good and considerate employers. The Leonard Cheshire Foundation, for instance, is in the *Sunday Times* list of top 20 best big employers, and six charities feature in its list of the 100 best employers in Britain.

HOW DOES THE VOLUNTARY SECTOR DIFFER FROM WORKING IN OTHER SECTORS?

Rosie Dick has experience of working both for a company and a charity. She is currently the Greater Manchester area co-ordinator for the Mentoring and Befriending Foundation and here she describes her experiences:

I worked for eight years at Barclay's Bank starting at a low level and moving up to team manager level in the private banking division. As I felt I couldn't get much more out of the job I jumped into the voluntary sector. The main difference between banking and my present position is that the work is less target driven and that you are left to 'drive your own train'. The work is altogether more creative and I am involved in a greater range of activities, including training, organising events and website design. On the debit side you feel more exposed financially. I have taken a drop in salary and because of funding uncertainties I am on a short term contract.

QUIZ: HOW MUCH DO YOU KNOW ABOUT THE VOLUNTARY SECTOR?

Here are some acronyms which denote organisations in the voluntary sector. Can you identify them and describe what they do?

- CAF

- DSC

- NCH

- NCVO

- NFP

- NGO

- NICVA

- NSPCC

- PDSA

- RNLI

- RSPN

- SCVO

- WWF

ANSWERS
CAF is the **Charities Aid Foundation,** a charity which assists the voluntary sector and donors by providing advice, banking facilities and other practical support.

DSC is the **Directory for Social Change** which publishes books and training manuals to support the voluntary sector. It also boasts a small but useful reference library at its London HQ.

NCH, formerly known as **National Care Homes,** was founded in 1869 and provides services for vulnerable and excluded children and young people. It is the leading provider of family and community centres and also provides services for young people leaving care.

NCVO is the **National Council for Voluntary Organisations**. It is an umbrella body for 4500 voluntary and community organisations in England and provides a wide range of information and support services. It also provides introductory courses to careers in charities (see Chapter 5).

NFP means **not for profit,** a term widely used in the USA and also in the UK to denote an organisation which is neither a business nor a branch of government.

NGO stands for **non-governmental organisation**. Many overseas aid charities, such as Oxfam and Actionaid, describe themselves as NGOs to show that they operate separately from national governments.

NICVA is the **Northern Ireland Council for Voluntary Action**, the equivalent of the NCVO in England, and a good source of information on volunteering in Ulster.

NSPCC is the **National Society for the Prevention of Cruelty to Children** which was founded in 1884 and has statutory powers that enable it to take action to safeguard children at risk of abuse. It employs 1800 staff and has 180 child protection teams nationwide.

PDSA is the **People's Dispensary for Sick Animals**, the leading veterinary charity founded in 1917 to provide free veterinary treatment and promote responsible pet ownership.

RNLI is the **Royal National Lifeboat Institution** founded in 1824 by Sir William Hillary. It provides life-saving services around the UK and Ireland and maintains 233 lifeboat stations.

RSPB is the **Royal Society for the Protection of Birds**, founded in 1889, and now the largest wildlife conservation charity in Europe. It maintains 182 nature reserves, has 1300 salaried staff and 130,000 volunteers.

SCVO is the **Scottish Council for Voluntary Organisations** and is the Scottish equivalent of the NCVO. It seeks to advance the values and interests of voluntary organisations in Scotland.

WWF stands for the **World Wildlife Fund**, the largest independent conservation organisation in the world operating in 90 countries to conserve endangered species, protect threatened habitats and address global threats.

CHAPTER 1

The truth about charity work

THE HISTORICAL BACKGROUND

The practice of charitable giving has a very long pedigree. We know that the Ancient Greeks and Romans gave to good causes, and in the Middle Ages individuals would donate money to public works, hospitals and the poor.

In 1601 the term 'charity' was given a legal definition when the first parliamentary Act was passed to regulate groups of individuals involved in philanthropic work. Three specific categories of charity were identified:

● The relief of poverty

● The advancement of education

● The advancement of religion.

Very often the charities were linked to the church and provided relief or schooling for the poor and needy. In old churches and civic institutions you sometimes find a list of charities and their benefactors, like this one in Cirencester Town Hall:

> The Blue School was erected in the Year 1714 principally by the Beneficence of Thomas Powell, Esq. and Rebecca, His Wife, for Cloathing and Educating forty poor Children. But before that Time several Sums of Money had been given for the Teaching of Children to Read, which were then appropriated to the Establishment of this Charity. My Powell, dying in 1718, left to the Charity £7 a Year and Half the Profits of Maskelyne's Ham in the Parish of Cricklade.

From the nineteenth century onwards the state began to play a bigger role in the provision of education and then welfare with the introduction of state pensions. The biggest change, however, came in the 1940s with the creation of the welfare state. This meant that the state took over the burden of responsibility for social welfare in the UK. However, there were gaps in state welfare provision and voluntary organisations found themselves continuing to play a significant role.

Voluntary organisations are often perceived as being more sensitive to particular needs as well as being more flexible and less hidebound by rules and regulations. As a result many now find themselves not only supplementing the activities of social service departments and the NHS but also being contracted to providing services on their behalf. One example of this is RNID's management of improvements to audiology services.

CHARITIES FIND A NEW ROLE

Charities, especially well established ones, don't remain static; they have to change with the times. Once such charity is Barnardo's which was founded by Dubliner Dr Thomas John Barnardo. Moved by the social deprivation he found in the East End of London, he set up a ragged school there in 1867, and in 1870 opened his first home for orphan boys in Stepney. A village home for 1500 girls in Barkingside came later, and by 1905, when Dr Barnardo died, his charity had 96 homes caring for some 8500 children.

Nowadays attitudes have changed and instead of putting children into homes it is considered more beneficial for them to be placed with families. The name has changed from Dr Barnardo's Homes to Barnardo's to reflect the changing role. The last Dr Barnardo's Home closed in 1989 and now the charity's efforts are concentrated on helping children within the community mainly through a network of family centres.

HOW MANY CHARITIES ARE THERE?

Currently there are over 167,000 organisations on the Charity Commission's Register, though many of them are them quite small. However, there are probably around 200,000 other organisations involved in 'good works' of some kind that are not registered with the Commission.

The reason for this is perfectly straightforward. Some of these organisations may not fulfil the strict criteria laid down by the Charities Commission, being political or campaigning organisations for instance. On the other hand the people running the charity might choose not to register.

Today charitable and voluntary institutions are classified into three main areas:

- The advancement of health; science, culture, arts and heritage; amateur sport; environmental protection and improvement

- The promotion of human rights, conflict resolution and reconciliation; animal welfare

- The provision of social housing; social and community advancement; other purposes beneficial to the community.

QUIZ: TRUE OR FALSE?

People have a number of misconceptions about charities and voluntary sector organisations. Can you separate the truth from fiction?

1. The welfare state has rendered charities superfluous.

2. Voluntary organisations exist only to help the poor.

3. The voluntary sector relies solely on volunteer help.

4. It is possible to make a career in the voluntary sector.

5. Charities are very laid-back, inefficient organisations.

6. Most charities have no paid staff at all.

7. Voluntary organisations pay peanuts so only mediocre people work for them.

ANSWERS

1. **FALSE**   Indeed, the government is keen to draw on the expertise of many voluntary organisations and pays some of them fees for services provided.

2. **FALSE**   They benefit other areas, such as the environment, the arts, cultural activities, animals, etc.

3. **FALSE**   Volunteers are very important with some 42% of the population volunteering at least once a year, but the sector also employs over 600,000 people on a salaried basis representing 2.2% of the working population.

4. **TRUE**   You can have a very good and worthwhile career in the voluntary sector either moving between organisations or achieving greater responsibility in just one.

5. **FALSE**   This may have been true in the past, but these days the voluntary sector has sharpened up its act to become more efficient and provide better value for money.

6. **TRUE**   Some of them are very small and therefore cannot afford to pay staff. Over half of them have annual incomes of £10,000 or less.

7. **FALSE**   Many charities have a reputation for being excellent employers providing reasonable (though not princely) pay packages and they attract some high calibre staff.

WHAT MAKES CHARITIES DIFFERENT?

In this book we consider charities and voluntary organisations together since there is usually a considerable overlap in how they are run. Both kinds of organisation have a philanthropic purpose even though not all of them will be registered with the Charities Commission. This may be out of choice or because they do not conform to the Commission's criteria. For example, Amnesty International and Liberty do not qualify because they have a political aim.

All charities and most voluntary organisations have the following features in common:

● They have been established to provide a public benefit, eg relief of poverty, advancement of education, other purposes beneficial to the community

● They are not designed to make a profit. Any surplus an organisation generates has to be ploughed back into the organisation

- They often rely heavily on volunteer help, though many (particularly the larger ones) have paid staff as well

- They are not under direct political control but are administered by a group of independent trustees.

Sometimes organisations of this nature use different terminology to describe themselves. For instance:

- **Third sector organisation:** ie not a businesses or public sector institution. This term would include friendly societies, professional organisations, trade unions and social enterprises

- **Not for profit organisation (NFP):** a term widely used in the USA to denote a third sector organisation

- **Non-governmental organisation (NGO):** a term used by many overseas aid charities.

WHAT IS A TYPICAL CHARITY LIKE?

There is no such thing as a typical charity or voluntary organisation. Some are enormous while others are very small. Some have a number of branches; others have just one large headquarters. Some are limited to a particular area, while others are national or international in scope.

The majority are small: over half of them – 56% – have an annual income of less than £10,000.

Roughly 19,000 have an annual income of between £100,000 and £1 million, 3000 or so earn between £1 million and £10 million, and almost 300 each generate an income of in excess of £10 million.

At the top end of the scale are 14 super-charities which each boast an income in excess of £100 million annually and account for 10% of the income of the voluntary sector. These are:

- Cancer Research UK

- The National Trust

- Oxfam

- NCH

- Barnardo's

- British Red Cross Society

- Royal Mencap Society

- British Heart Foundation

- Leonard Cheshire Foundation

- Save the Children

- Royal National Lifeboat Institution

- NSPCC

- Salvation Army

- Scope.

These organisations have become household words because of their need to maintain a high profile and attract plenty of donations.

WHERE DOES THE MONEY COME FROM?

A business makes its money by manufacturing goods or providing services which it sells in order to make a profit. The government (including government agencies and local government) derives its income from the taxes it levies on each one of us, in the form of income tax, council tax, VAT, vehicle tax, excise duty, etc.

The factor that distinguishes the voluntary sector from all others is that it receives grants and donations from individuals and trusts for its work. However, this is beginning to change. Some charities derive some of their income from selling goods and services, through their own high street shops and mail order catalogues for instance. Currently the amount of earned income over the charity sector as a whole (£12.5 billion) exceeds the amount of voluntary income (£11.8 billion). This suggests that some charities are becoming more like the private sector in the techniques they employ to raise income.

Another source of funding is the public sector. The latest estimates from the NCVO put this at over £10 billion; a figure that includes income from lottery distributors and overseas governments, as well as the government and local councils. The state now accounts for 38% of the revenues of the voluntary sector.

Although the state is a major source of revenue, individual donations remain important. Almost 60% of UK adults give to charity in a typical month, the average donation being over £14.

WHAT IS THE SCOPE OF THE VOLUNTARY SECTOR?

There are charities and voluntary organisation which cater for nearly every need. Here are some of the major categories:

- Animals
- The armed services
- Children
- Cultural
- The disabled
- The elderly
- Family welfare
- The environment
- Heritage
- Hospices
- Law and order
- Maritime
- Medical research
- Medical welfare
- Overseas aid
- Social welfare
- Young people.

QUIZ: HOW MANY CHARITIES CAN YOU NAME?

How many charities can you think of for each category? This book has already mentioned some of them. Charity Trends (the book or the website: www.cafonline.org), the Guidestar UK website (www.guidestar.org.uk) or the Charities Direct website (www.charitiesdirect.com) will prove a useful research tool.

ANSWERS

As we have seen there are around 400,000 voluntary organisations and it is impossible to list them all in this slim volume. Many of them will be local charities, which are involved in work every bit as important as high profile national charities but are probably unknown outside their local area.

Animals

Charities devoted to animal welfare range from large national ones such as the RSPCA to animal shelters and wildlife groups that serve a restricted locality. Here are a few names: Battersea Dogs' Home, Blue Cross, Cats Protection, Compassion in World Farming, The Donkey Sanctuary, International Fund for Animal Welfare, League Against Cruel Sports, Rare Breeds Survival Trust, RSPB, RSPCA, WWF.

The armed services

Of the many charities for serving and former service personnel the Royal British Legion, famous for its Poppy Appeal in November, is the best known. Others are the RAF Benevolent Fund, the Royal Naval Benevolent Fund, SSAFA Forces Help and a number of charities attached to particular regiments.

Children

Among the national charities the best known are probably Barnardo's, Childline, Great Ormond Street Children's Trust, NCH, NSPCC, Save the Children UK and SOS Children's Villages. In addition to these there are thousands of others, some of which receive funding from the annual BBC Children in Need appeal.

Cultural

There is a wide range of organisations ranging from small local arts organisations to The Royal Opera House and Victoria and Albert Museum, both of which have fundraising departments. Many theatres, including the Royal Shakespeare Theatre, are registered charities, and so are orchestras, such as the City of Birmingham Symphony Orchestra, and organisations providing encouragement and support for young artists, such as the Young Artists' Concert Trust. While many of the smaller charities rely solely on volunteers, others employ arts administrators and fundraisers to support performances and exhibitions by arts practitioners.

The disabled

There seem to be charities for almost every disability. They include the British Polio Fellowship, Guide Dogs for the Blind, Leonard Cheshire, which provides residential homes, drop in centres and respite care, Queen Elizabeth's Foundation for Disabled People, Royal National Institute for the Deaf, Scope, the Treloar Trust, and Thrive, a charity which promotes gardening skills among the disabled.

The elderly

Age Concern and Help the Aged are among the most prominent charities in this sector, and both of them have a large number of local branches. Others include Aid for the Aged in Distress and the Abbeyfield Society which provides care and housing for older people.

Environment

This sector brings together a wide range of organisations which campaign and work for a better environment. Some of the best known names are the BTCV (formerly the British Trust for Conservation Volunteers), Earthwatch, Friends of the Earth, Greenpeace, the Marine Conservation Society, the Ramblers' Association, the Wildfowl and Wetlands Trust and Woodland Heritage. Many localities have their own local wildlife trust which is essentially an all-volunteer affair.

Family welfare
Relate is an organisation which counsels partners whose marriage is in difficulties. Cruse Bereavement Care and the Compassionate Friends offer bereavement counselling, and a number of children's charities, such as Barnardo's, help families which are facing difficulties. Carers UK is a charity which gives advice to people who have to look after (usually) a family member.

Heritage
The National Trust is the UK's second largest charity in terms of income, and there are a number of others, such as the Georgian Society and the Victorian Society which endeavour to preserve Britain's architectural treasures. The Civic Trust has a network of (mainly) voluntary organisations throughout the UK, and there are others such as the British Waterways Trust and Save Britain's Heritage.

Hospices
The Hospice Movement started in 1967 with the establishment of St Christopher's Hospice in Sydenham, South London. Many areas now have their own hospices offering residential care and house visits for the terminally ill. In addition to employing medical staff they also employ their own fundraisers. For further information on hospices contact the Hospice Information Service at St Christopher's. There is also a national charity, Help the Hospices.

Law and order
The Prison Fellowship and NACRO help with the rehabilitation of offenders and provide support. Organisations, such as the Howard League and Prison Reform Trust campaign for prison reform, while Victims Support provides help to those who have been victims of crime. In addition, many independent law centres, funded by grants and voluntary contributions, operate across the land.

Maritime
There are a number of organisations which look after the interests of seafarers and retired seafarers, including the

British and International Sailors Society, the King George's Fund for Sailors, the Merchant Navy Welfare Board, the Seaman's Hospital Society and Trinity House. The RNLI provides rescue services while the Marine Society provides educational facilities for seafarers and careers advice to young people planning a life at sea.

Medical research

Medical research attracts one of the largest proportions of voluntary donations of any sector with Cancer Research leading the way. The British Heart Foundation, Cancer UK, the Cystic Fibrosis Trust, the King's Fund and the Mental Health Foundation are among the best known, but there are several smaller regional ones, such as the Yorkshire Cancer Trust. The Association of Medical Research Charities can supply a list of its 114 members.

Medical welfare

A range of organisations could be mentioned in this category, including some of those mentioned above. Mind and the Royal MENCAP Society are very active with people suffering from a mental handicap. Alcoholics Anonymous speaks for itself, while Addaction is a national charity which tackles drug addiction. Macmillan Nurses and Marie Curie Cancer Care provide support for cancer patients, while ASH and QUIT encourage smokers to quit.

Overseas aid

Overseas aid remains one of the most popular causes and many of the charities in this sector are household names thanks to their regular appeals. The bigger ones include Action Aid, the British Red Cross, Christian Aid, Médecins Sans Frontières, MERLIN (a medical charity), Oxfam, Save the Children, World Vision, while there are smaller ones like the International Refugee Trust. There are also a number of organisations which send people on voluntary placements abroad, such as VSO and i-to-i.

Politics and campaigning

The political parties are essentially voluntary organisations, even though they are not classed as charities. There are many other organisations that campaign for better conditions and lobby governments, such as Anti-Slavery International, the Campaign Against Drinking and Driving, the Campaign for Nuclear Disarmament (CND), the Child Poverty Action Group and the Howard League for Penal Reform.

Social welfare

Organisations, such as the British Refugee Council and Refugee Action provide assistance to refugees and there are a number of charities dedicated to the welfare of different ethnic groups. Shelter and Crisis highlight the problems of the homeless and provide some solutions; Victim Support provides support for the victims of crime. The Salvation Army continues to be active in a number of social welfare fields.

Young people

The Prince's Trust comes into this category and offers support and encouragement to young people who face barriers to success. The ubiquitous YMCA and YWCA offer training and counselling to young people well as hostel and recreational activities. The Youth Action Network encourages people to go on projects overseas while Young Enterprise gives people practical encouragement to work in industry.

How did you do?

The number of different charities is bewildering and you may find it difficult to choose which one you would like to work for. However, it may be easier to make your choice on the basis of a particular type of job, and the next chapter will deal review the types of employment on offer.

CHAPTER 2

Jobs in charities

The range of charities and voluntary organisations, as you have seen, is enormous. The same applies to the range of jobs in this sector, and the term charity worker could cover a wide range of job categories.

Most of the people working in the voluntary sector are volunteers, including the trustees of charities. However, some of the jobs in charities require people who can devote more time than just a few hours or one day a week, and this is where paid staff come in.

WHAT KIND OF JOBS ARE THEY?

Have a look at the list below.

- Accountant
- Administrator
- Adviser
- Arts development officer

- Campaigns manager
- Caseworker
- Community worker
- Conservation officer

- Director/CEO
- Development officer
- Estate manager
- Facilities manager
- Finance director
- Fundraiser
- General manager
- Housing officer
- Human resources manager
- Information, policy and research assistant
- Instructor
- IT expert
- Marketing officer
- Nurse
- Overseas development worker
- Personnel officer
- Procurement officer
- Project worker
- Public relations officer
- Receptionist
- Shop manager
- Secretary
- Social worker
- Solicitor
- Support worker
- Technician
- Therapist
- Training officer
- Volunteer co-ordinator.

WHICH OF THESE JOBS WOULD YOU EXPECT TO FIND IN THE CHARITY SECTOR?

The short answer is: all of them. Not that every charity will offer the whole range of jobs. Charities often require people with particular skills to deliver the benefits they offer. A legal centre will require solicitors, but is unlikely to need a conservation officer on its staff.

An animal shelter may need a volunteer co-ordinator but not a housing officer. The National Trust is unlikely to need social workers but may well need estate managers. A youth charity might well employ instructors or advisers, but not an arts development officer.

Even so the range of jobs, certainly in a larger charity, can be extensive. As this book was being written, for example, the homeless charity Shelter was advertising the following vacancies in different parts of the country:

- Children and young person's team leader

- Housing advice caseworker

- Homelessness prevention officer

- Area manager

- Artist and celebrity liaison manager

- Head of research

- Corporate account manager

- Housing adviser

- Building surveyor

- Head of media

- Refugee community training and development worker.

In addition the charity had vacancies for volunteer support workers – an excellent way of getting experience.

THE MAIN JOB AREAS

You may have found the list at the beginning of this chapter confusing or even overwhelming. So let's try to simplify matters by considering them under four main headings:

- Management and administration

- Delivery of a benefit

- Volunteer recruitment and support

- Fundraising.

MANAGEMENT AND ADMINISTRATION
Every organisation has to be managed. If you serve on the
executive committee of a club, for instance, you will know that you
and your fellow committee members are responsible for running
the club efficiently, ensuring that it functions according to its
stated aims, drawing up a budget and keeping to it, recruiting
staff, keeping within the law, paying the bills, monitoring customer
satisfaction, making financial and policy decisions, etc. A
management function is found in all organisations. In some, the
work is done by just one person; in larger organisations it is
spread among the CEO (chief executive officer), the finance
director, company secretary and the communications officer
assisted by accountants, marketing managers, personnel officers,
PAs, secretaries and receptionists.

DELIVERY OF A BENEFIT
Many voluntary organisations have been set up to render a service,
usually to a particular clientele, though in some cases they raise
funds which they pass on to other organisations to do the work for
them (see Case Study 1).

The clientele could be ex-prisoners, drug addicts, elderly people,
disadvantaged youngsters, ex-prisoners, people with an acute
illness, the homeless, people in debt, etc. Animals, too benefit from
the activities of charities, such as the RSPCA.

The people delivering the service are variously described as
advisers, project officers, welfare officers, support workers, case
workers, therapists, community workers, etc. Many of them have
their equivalents in the public sector and in many cases specialist
skills or training are required. So you have charity workers who
rehabilitate drug addicts, assist refugees with their problems, offer
advice on benefits and legal matters, provide relief to disaster

victims, counsel people with emotional difficulties or help to house homeless people.

Some charities do not help individuals in this way. Their aim is to heighten awareness: of the dangers of smoking, of ways to prevent accidents in the home, of the problems of Third World debt, of the plight of political prisoners, etc. Their staff have to be educators and people with verbal and written skills. Others aim to bring pressure on governments and other powerful institutions to change the law or make better provision for minorities.

Conservation charities benefit the general public more indirectly. Their attention is based on preserving the environment, maintaining wildlife sanctuaries, preserving old buildings, etc, and have a need for people with practical, less people-oriented skills. There are also many arts based charities which aim to provide high quality arts events or encourage people to become involved in the arts, perhaps in order to overcome a major handicap.

Charities vary considerably their aims and the people they aim to benefit. As a result the sector can offer a varied range of job opportunities, both on a volunteer and a salaried basis (see especially Case Study 2).

VOLUNTEER RECRUITMENT AND SUPPORT

In many cases the service delivery is performed by volunteers under the guidance of full-time staff. Some charities have staff dedicated to recruiting and supporting the volunteers (see Case Study 3). These are often called volunteer co-ordinators, volunteer support officers or volunteer managers and their duty is to motivate volunteers, train them, if necessary, allocate them to suitable projects or people, and monitor their progress. If the volunteers are likely to deal with children or vulnerable people, legislation may require checks into a person's background.

Many areas have a volunteer bureau with just one salaried employee who is actively engaged with a number of organisations requiring volunteers and needs to evaluate their projects in order to assess their suitability for volunteers. The person may also need to attract volunteers by holding recruitment events or perhaps manning a stall at a recruitment fair. Good person to person skills are needed as some volunteers may be unsure of themselves and have taken on this role to achieve a sense of self-esteem. Some volunteers, for instance, may have been made redundant or have experienced a recent problem in their lives and need to be dealt with carefully.

A volunteer co-ordinator therefore needs to be something of a diplomat. It is not like dealing with paid staff, who are obliged to observe the disciplines of the workplace. Volunteers can come and go as they like and need to be cosseted rather than cajoled.

FUNDRAISING

One feature of charities, which differentiates them from organisations in the public or private sector, is fundraising. Its importance can be gauged from the number of advertisements that appear for fundraising vacancies. On one charity careers website some 40% vacancies were directly related to this activity. While some charities may delegate this task to professional fundraisers, the majority keep their fundraising in-house. Without funds the charity is unable to finance its work, and the more successful its fundraising is the more it can achieve (see Case Studies 1 and 4).

FUNDRAISING IN FOCUS

Because so many jobs in charities are involved with fundraising we need to find out how it really works. It involves far more than appealing for funds in newspapers and organising street collections, although such activities do bring in a considerable amount of income.

Raising cash is far more wide-reaching than that, and fundraisers employ a wide range of strategies to secure funding. While a small charity may employ just one or two people to do this task, larger ones have specialists working in different fields. These are shown below.

FUNDRAISING FROM TRUSTS AND FOUNDATIONS

There are thousands of grant-making trusts with money to give out to fund charitable activities, and the amount of money they give away annually totals some £2 billion, which is far more than companies and individuals give. The Wellcome Trust, the Nuffield Foundation and the Joseph Rowntree Charitable Trust are among the largest and best known, while at the other end of the scale there are local trusts with perhaps only a few thousand pounds at their disposal. The biggest in the world is the Bill and Melinda Gates Foundation established by the founder of Microsoft. This kind of fundraising is regarded as the most useful kind of fundraising since it is particularly cost-effective. Trust fundraisers have the job of identifying which trusts and foundations are likely to be favourably disposed to their particular charity and applying to them.

FUNDRAISING FROM STATUTORY BODIES

This is in many respects similar to trust fundraising, except that the fund providers are from the public sector ranging from government departments (such as the Department of Health) to local councils which often give grants to community arts associations, community law centres and citizens advice bureaux. Funds generated by income from the National Lottery are becoming very important.

CORPORATE FUNDRAISING

Here the charity creates a relationship between itself and a particular company to generate income through employee fundraising, payroll giving (encouraging monthly donations from employees), joint promotions or a straight donation. This is a popular and high profile means of raising money, though it does not result in large amounts. This is sometimes described as **business development** and **account management**.

COMMUNITY FUNDRAISING

This involves encouraging local groups of volunteers and supporters to raise money for your particular charity as part of a local initiative or sometimes as part of a national campaign. Where no such support group exists in a particular area community fundraisers have the task of creating one and supporting it through liaison with local schools, Rotary Clubs, etc. Community fundraisers are also called **fundraising managers** and **regional fundraisers**.

EVENTS

The London Marathon is a good example of an event that raises millions of pounds though sponsorship for charity. But there are many others; anything from sponsored parachute jumping to a celebrity golf tournament. This often involves recruiting and managing volunteers and perhaps working with special events organisers. Imagination and good organisational skills are required for which good organisational flair is required.

INDIVIDUAL GIVING
Individual donations raise large amounts for charities, and you probably receive invitations through the post on a regular basis to contribute to this or that charity. Through these mailings charities hope to encourage people to give on a regular basis, and the means used are becoming more sophisticated. One aspect of this is encouraging people to leave a legacy to the charity when they pass on.

MAJOR DONOR FUNDRAISING
This is a growing aspect of fundraising whereby charities target wealthy individuals to give generously and in turn introduce their wealthy friends to the charity.

TRADING VENTURES
A number of the larger charities earn income through the sale of Christmas cards and other items and the profits are ploughed back into the charity. These are sold both through mail order catalogues and charity shops, which can be found in every high street. Although the latter are normally staffed by volunteers, they are supported by teams of area and regional managers who recruit volunteers and monitor sales.

MARKETING AND PR
There is a strong link between fundraising and marketing and PR. The aim is to keep the profile of the charity high and keep it in the public eye through press reports of its activities. Organisations and individuals need to be kept informed about a charity's activities through advertisements, press releases, interviews, newsletters and annual reports; one important reason being that it may encourage them to give more (see Case Study 5).

JOB DESCRIPTIONS

This section consists of typical job advertisements across the whole spectrum of the charitable/voluntary sector. Some of them require people with specific experience and qualifications, while others are entry level positions.

Read through each one and try to work out:

- What does the job entail?

- What type of person does the charity want?

- What qualifications are needed?

- Does the job appeal to you?

- What training and experience would you need for it?

- Have you the right kind of personality for the job?

OFFICE MANAGER

We are looking for an experienced administrator to join our highly motivated, friendly and growing team of professionals based at our busy head office. As the first point of contact for telephone enquiries and visitors a pleasant telephone manner and friendly demeanour is essential.

Working closely with the office manager/PA to the chief operating officer, you will be responsible for much of the day to day administration in the office as well as provide administrative support to other teams. This role will therefore require a highly organised and flexible approach to your work.

The role is ideally suited to an individual who enjoys working in a busy office environment, with good communication and team skills. A sound working knowledge of MS Office is essential, as well as a proven track record of multitasking effectively. You must be willing to undertake training to further develop your computer skills and learn new packages. Accurate typing skills with an attention to detail are naturally essential.

FUNDRAISING RESEARCHER

A leading care and research charity is seeking experienced and exceptionally talented individuals to join our fundraising team.

Working with the development manager and wider fundraising team you will play a pivotal role within the department by undertaking and managing research which will include individuals, trusts, corporates, charity trends, markets and techniques. You will need good organisational, communication, analytical and presentation skills, at least two years' experience of prospect fundraising or market research, and have knowledge of MS Office packages and fundraising databases. Knowledge of market research packages and data protection regulation is desired.

CAMPAIGNS AND MARKETING ADMINISTRATOR

We are looking for an efficient and motivated individual to support the work of our campaigns and marketing team.

You will provide administrative backup for the department's staff as well as support on key marketing projects. Duties will include co-ordinating delivery of the charity's publications, setting up internal and external meetings and helping to prepare presentations as well as booking travel and accommodation, data entry, filing, dealing with correspondence and occasional reception work.

You will also be responsible for conducting desk research, and liaising with design agencies and suppliers. You must also be IT literate, familiar with MS Office and committed to equality and diversity.

MAJOR DONOR FUNDRAISER

The fundraising division of this charity is made up of four teams: Employee and Community Events, Business Development, Major Gifts (from trusts and major individuals) and Direct Marketing (donor recruitment and appeals).

High-level donors are an increasingly vital part of our direct marketing plans. Therefore, the direct marketing team manager's job is to devise and implement strategies in order to identify and recruit new high-level donors and to ensure the section meets agreed income targets. They also need to develop and nurture relationships with major donors in order to maximise long-term income.

Two years' experience in fundraising and direct marketing is the minimum requirement for this job, as the ability to analyse and report on the performance of campaigns as well as manage budgets and databases is essential to its success. Excellent skills in customer relations and collaborative team working are also needed.

AREA FUNDRAISING MANAGER

We are looking for an exceptional individual to fill a key post within our Northern Territory Fundraising Team. We need an area fundraising manager to work with staff and volunteers to maximise fundraising income.

Managing fundraising activity including volunteers, events and corporate fundraising you will give hands-on support to your team and take personal responsibility for fundraising initiatives.

We are looking for a dynamic and enthusiastic fundraiser with experience of managing people, a track record of delivering fundraising results, excellent written and verbal communication skills, excellent planning and budgeting skills, and two years' fundraising experience

MEMBERSHIP SERVICES MANAGER

We are a charity working to represent the views and expectations of over 10 million disabled people to influence legislative reform and social change. We are looking for an experienced, self-motivated individual to manage, develop and strengthen our membership services. Responsibilities include recruiting new members, and retaining and building relationships with current members. In addition you will organise regular visits to members around the charity to establish and develop collaborative relationships. Some travel and out of hours work will be required.

TRAINEE POSITION

This development charity offers an opportunity for a trainee to work for a year with our office. The programme will offer the trainee the chance to work within a high profile development and relief agency in programme development. The programme is designed to give individuals practical experience in different locations around the world in preparation for a possible career in international development. During the year you will work eight months in our UK office and approximately four months with our partner offices in developing countries.

ACTIVITIES CO-ORDINATOR

This charity provides guidance, training and work experience to enable people disadvantaged by poor mental health to fulfil their potential. The position involves motivating, supervising and coaching clients to undertake commercially oriented work to engage in creative/therapeutic activities while maintaining a positive, safe and supportive environment. It will require lots of energy and initiative and a creative approach.

The ability to initiate and develop new activities, develop relationships with existing and new commercial customers and liaise with clients' care teams are all essential. An excellent communicator with strong supervisory, organisational, admin, IT and team working skills, you will also be able to work with clients on a one to one basis or in groups, providing additional support to those who are able to progress towards mainstream employment and training.

PROJECT SUPPORT ASSISTANT

This is a multilingual housing advice project that addresses the housing needs of everyone in the area, but particularly focuses on the needs of those from the ethnic communities. Handling your own caseload of tenants you will provide practical and emotional support that will help them to become established in their home and community. With an in-depth understanding of local community issues you need to be comfortable working with a range of agencies and groups and speak a community language such as Sylheti or Bengali.

NATIONAL VOLUNTEERING CO-ORDINATOR

We are looking for someone to develop and drive forward our national volunteering strategy, to make sure our valued and diverse volunteer workforce is the best it can be to meet the needs of the victims and witnesses we help.

You must have previous experience of service delivery and of managing volunteer recruitment and retention programmes, You must also have good knowledge of the motivations behind volunteering and of current volunteering promotion initiatives. A strong understanding of the importance of diversity and a commitment to equal opportunities are important.

MONEY ADVICE CASEWORKER

We are seeking two highly motivated people to be part of an exciting new project aimed at increasing debt advice provision in the area.

Applicants must have a minimum of two years' full-time (or part-time equivalent) recent experience of providing a casework service in the field of debt; experience of court work in relation to debt; excellent communication skills; driving licence and the use of a car.

DIRECTOR

We are an arts in education charity which organises visits and workshops from children's writers, poets and dramatists. Having grown from a small voluntary group, we now work with over 25,000 children every year in primary and secondary schools, as well as special needs schools and pupil referral units. We have also done outreach work in prisons, care homes, hospitals and with social services. Our strategic plan is now to expand the programme and so we need a new director to enable an expansion in the charity's fundraising performance, and increase our local and regional profile in line with our current levels of activity.

HOME SUPPORT WORKER

We are looking for a self-motivated, proactive, enthusiastic team player for this post. The post holder will support people with learning disabilities who live independently in their own homes. This hands-on support will be to enable them to maintain their tenancy and homes and to empower them to take control of their own lives.

The successful applicant must have excellent written and verbal communication skills, and must be qualified to NVQ level 2 in Care (or equivalent). They must possess a full driving licence and have access to a vehicle. Applicants must have a professional and versatile outlook, with the ability to manage their own workload, and extensive knowledge of the many and complex issues faced by people with learning disabilities. They must be able to work on their own initiative and unsupervised and be able to motivate and support service users. One year's prior experience of people with a learning disability, either as part of paid employment or in a non-paid capacity, is essential, as is an awareness of current good practice relating to a service for people with learning disabilities.

EMPLOYMENT ADVISER

To deliver guidance and advice services currently defined through contracts to work with the National Probation Service/London Probation Area.

To work towards achieving the objectives and standards as set out in the business plan

To increase the employment prospects of clients by providing information advice and guidance on education, training and employment opportunities.

To promote awareness of the education, training and employment needs of ex-offenders and the benefits of this type of active intervention.

The guidance worker will assess the training and development needs of individual clients and provide each with a personal plan of action to meet these needs; refer clients to appropriate training and development programmes; assist in the production of CVs and the completion of application forms; and actively use and contribute to all organisation's resources: paper and IT based.

SALARIES AND WORKING CONDITIONS

Salaries will differ according to the size of the organisation and the amount of responsibility that goes with the job. Starting salaries can vary between £12,000 and £21,000 according to a recent survey. The amount will depend on the location of the job, the charity in question and the nature of the work.

A large number of charities are based in London and the South East, and this is where many of the jobs are. However, the larger charities have regional and local offices all around the country. If you do not wish to live in London, it would be worthwhile investigating local charities in your particular area.

Salaries in London tend to be higher than elsewhere to reflect the higher living costs; smaller charities tend, on the whole, to offer less to their employees than larger ones; and fundraisers tend to earn more than other staff, because they are in short supply. Senior positions attract more remuneration packages and salaries in the £40,000–£60,000 range are attainable. The most senior posts would offer up to £80,000.

Here are examples of typical salaries being offered in 2006.

- Accounts assistant, London: £9–£10 per hour

- Activities co-ordinator, London: £20,300–£23,800

- Administrator, Wales: £9,000

- Campaigns and policy officer, North: £22,400

- Community fundraiser, Essex: £18,500–£22,500

- Direct marketing co-ordinator, London: £24,000–£26,000

- Director, arts organisation: £25,000

- Homeless officer, London: £16–£18 per hour

- Officer junior, London: £11,000

- Policy and research manager, London: £34,000

- Project worker, homeless charity, London: £24,700–£27,800

- Support and advocacy worker, South West: £20,000

- Volunteer bureau manager, West, £12,000.

CASE STUDIES
In the following section four people working in the charity voluntary sector talk about themselves and their jobs.

CASE STUDY 1
Ros Wild is the administrator of International Refugee Trust, which raises money to fund refugee projects in the Third World.

I had worked in PR and for a media company for many years and decided I wanted to do something on a smaller scale and where I would be more useful to the wider world. Then I saw an ad in the local paper for the position of administrator at IRT. I decided to apply, was offered the job and have now been here for four years.

Working for a small charity is quite different from life in the business world. The pressures are different. In business the pressures revolved around making money for shareholders. At IRT the pressure is constantly making sure we have raised sufficient funds for our projects.

The sums of money involved at IRT are far smaller than those in business and it seems more like real life. We receive donations from a wide variety of people who take a real interest in our work. This means the work has much more of a personal feel and you feel out of the rat race.

Since we are a small office of only three staff, the work is very varied. Today, for instance, I was supervising the despatch of the newsletter, which I had written myself, to our supporters. I had to check that transfers to projects overseas have been made and acknowledged. I had to discuss with the auditor the part of our annual report concerned with restricted funds since I have special responsibility for these funds and need to ensure that they are sent to the projects they are earmarked for. I also had to send off promotional materials to a group of supporters who want to raise money for us.

IRT is a small charity, which raises about £500,000 a year. We have a niche position among overseas aid charities in that we are involved in small scale projects, many of them run by missionary sisters, and we do not employ any staff overseas. Sometimes we give grants of just a few hundred pounds, but it can make a huge difference to the organisation concerned.

Nowadays working for a charity has become the 'flavour of the month' and it is getting increasingly difficult to land a position if you are at the beginning of your career. So newcomers need to try to enter at any level. However, the sector suffers from a shortage of fundraisers.

CASE STUDY 2

Nicola Schofield is the manager of Bully Free Zone, a small charity based in Bolton which offers information and support to young people and families who are affected by bullying.

I became involved in the voluntary sector while I was studying for a degree in Community Studies at Bolton Institute where I helped out at the welfare advice centre. On graduation I worked for an insurance company and a mortgage company for a bit, but I found the private sector gave me no sense of purpose so I decided to move on.

I started off as a support worker with Bully Free Zone as a way into the voluntary sector. I have been with the organisation for six years – apart from a short period working for the local authority – and am now the manager of the project. I have overall responsibility for staff management, financial matters, securing funding and promoting the organisation. We have five staff members and 200 trained Millennium Volunteers who offer peer support to victims of bullying.

Most of our funding comes in the form of grants from trusts, such as Children in Need and Comic Relief, plus the occasional donation. The main problem with funding is that nobody wants to fund core costs; they want to fund new initiatives.

I like the job because it gives me a sense of satisfaction from helping other people. It also offers flexibility, not only in achieving a good work–life balance but also in the things you do. I am forever on the look-out for new projects. It also offers variety; every day is different. I could be working in the office one day, out working on a project the next and then perhaps attending a meeting.

I need challenges and in this organisation you have scope for development. So long as I can see the organisation moving forward, I would like to stay with it. If I do move on I would like to continue working in the voluntary sector on community-based projects.

The disadvantage of the job involves money. There is always uncertainty as to how long the job will last because the funding might end. Some charities offer good staff benefits to balance out the low pay they offer.

CASE STUDY 3

Ian Parker is a friendship scheme co-ordinator for the Guideposts Trust in Gloucestershire, a charity that offers support to all vulnerable adults and children.

In the South West region we now support over one thousand individuals who I believe receive a positive service from well-qualified and experienced staff.

My job involves pairing adults with learning difficulties with volunteers with similar interests. I like to meet both sides face to face in order to explain how the friendship scheme operates, and I usually accompany them on their initial meetings to ensure that everything is working out.

I actually graduated with a degree in Sports Management from the University of Plymouth. While I was still a student I worked for the local borough council as a playscheme leader during the summer. After graduation I spent the summer coordinating a large activities programme for 11–16 year olds, again for the council.

My first permanent job was working as an out of school fieldworker for the charity PATA (Parents and Toddlers Association). This involved helping the owners and organisers of out of school clubs and giving them advice on running their club.

Although this was a full-time job, I only worked during term-time, so for the summer vacation I applied to Guideposts Unlimited, the branch of the Guideposts Trust that organises challenging activities for people with learning activities. I worked with them as an assistant organiser. It was at this time that I heard the local friendship scheme co-ordinator of the Trust left creating a vacancy, so I applied for the job and was lucky enough to be offered it.

Working for a charity like this is quite similar to working for the borough council, in the sense that there is no requirement to make money. Being able to help people makes my work worthwhile and at the same time I am learning new skills.

One snag is that because the charity has expanded so rapidly in the past five years the systems are not keeping pace with the growth and communication difficulties sometimes occur. My main problem is finding enough volunteers to pair off with my clients, so I have to market the scheme to potential volunteers.

Finding clients is not hard; they either contact me themselves or are referred to me by a friend, a family member or social services. Every month I have supervision sessions with my line manager, the deputy service manager for the region, and we discuss any problems I might be facing.

Our scheme is a new one and is funded by the Community Fund of the National Lottery. Although its future is not completely secure, if I can prove the worth of the scheme it will continue.

There is no real opportunity for career progression in my current area in this charity, but that doesn't bother me at present since I'm not looking to go anywhere. Eventually, however, I may need to move on.

CASE STUDY 4
Ruth Mantle works as a fundraiser for The Refugee Council in London. Her job title is Institutional Giving Officer.

During university and after graduation, I worked as a temp in a number of different companies, the Home Office, the Department of Culture Media and Sport, for an MP at the House of Commons and a voluntary organisation. As a result of this experience I decided I felt most motivated by the voluntary sector. However, it was not easy getting into the sector as I found there was great competition for entry-level jobs for recent graduates. I applied for numerous vacancies over the year and decided I was pitching myself too high.

I finally got my first paid job after doing fundraising work for a voluntary organisation. I started working as a fundraiser for Raleigh International applying to charitable trusts, the government and the EU for funding. The initial contract was for five months but this was extended to a permanent contract and I worked there for a year and a half. This was a rollercoaster of a job for me since I was originally in a team of four and ended up as sole fundraiser.

For my next step I wanted to work for a larger charity and in a team. My job with the Refugee Council fitted perfectly. This proved to be a steep learning curve, since this is a job where you have to be really on the ball. Fundraising for a charity is not a nice easy option; in fact, you have to work incredibly hard.

A fundraiser does not work in isolation. We have to build up good relations not only with donors but also with the project staff since they have the project and specialist knowledge that we couldn't fundraise without.

One of the things I like about working for a charity is that my fellow workers, like me, are passionate about what we are doing. We all share the same values, and I know exactly who I am working to benefit. However, many people do not see working in the voluntary sector as a career, though as fundraisers are becoming more professional it has now started to be regarded as one.

Due to their specialist knowledge and skills fundraisers' salaries tend to be higher than those of other workers in the voluntary sector. However, your pay is still lower than the private sector and will not increase in the same way over your career.

One challenge that small to medium charities face is finding the funds to invest in staff development. It is difficult to justify these costs to trustees and donors, even though they have a direct benefit for the charity and its beneficiaries. However, there are a few charitable trusts that offer bursaries for staff working in the voluntary sector to undertake professional training.

In a typical working day I would:

● Research organisations to see how much they might give and whether they would favour any particular projects

● Maintain relationships with donors keeping them informed of our progress

● Write applications and proposals to potential donors

● Keep up to date with projects and areas of work that need funding.

I could do most of this from the office, but I like to network and talk to people face to face, which is a more effective method than simply writing a letter or making a phone call. Donors and potential donors are given the chance to visit our work and see it for themselves.

CHAPTER 3

Routes into paid jobs in the voluntary sector

Now that you have had a chance to look at some of the charities and the range of jobs they offer, it is time to take stock and decide

- What are you looking for in a job?

- Does the voluntary sector offer what you are looking for?

- What kind of organisation would suit you?

- Are you suited to this kind of work?

- What can you offer a voluntary sector employer?

WHAT ARE YOU LOOKING FOR IN A JOB?

Job expectations differ from person to person and you need to consider what you want from a particular job or your career as a whole. It is better to find a job that you feel comfortable with than one which sounds fine on paper but does not reflect your aspirations.

Look at the following list. Which of these aspirations do you share?

● **Achievement:** I want to face challenges and achieve results

● **Autonomy:** I prefer to work independently of others

● **High earnings:** I need a good salary will in order to enjoy a high standard of living

● **Job satisfaction:** I want to be happy and comfortable in the job that I am doing

● **Outdoor life:** I would like a job where I spend a large part of my time out of doors

● **Responsibility:** I am keen to take responsibility and be in a position of leadership

● **Security:** I want a secure job with an organisation which will look after me well

● **Self-development:** I am keen to acquire different skills in order to advance in my career

● **Self-expression:** I need opportunities to be creative and use my personality to good effect

● **Social relevance:** I want the opportunity to meet with and help other people

● **Status:** I would like a high profile position which offers me plenty of prestige

● **Variety:** I am seeking the chance to deploy a range of skills within a variety of contexts.

WHAT CAN THE VOLUNTARY SECTOR OFFER?

The voluntary sector can fulfil some of these expectations in full or in part, but it cannot fulfil all of them. Let us examine each of them in turn to work out which ones are a match.

Achievement   This is certainly possible if you are with a successful charity. You can get a feeling of achievement from managing a project successfully, initiating a new one or achieving fundraising targets. And you often see the results of your work.

Autonomy   Charities tend to be a team effort. However some of the smaller ones, in particular, need people who are capable of working on their own without very much direction.

High earnings   If you want a six or seven figure salary, look elsewhere. Most voluntary sector staff earn considerably less than they would in commerce. Although the top jobs in larger charities pay well, they compare unfavourably with the private sector.

Job satisfaction   People working in the voluntary sector normally have a high level of job satisfaction knowing that they are doing work of benefit to the community.

Outdoor life   Some charities, including some working with animals and the environment, offer a chance to get out of the office and meet clients. But this will depend very much on the nature of the job.

Responsibility   On the whole charities need people who are prepared to take responsibility. This is particularly true of small charities and those which are widely dispersed.

Security   A large number of jobs in charities, particular smaller ones, are dependent on funding and tend to be on a short-term contract basis. Although some benefits may be on offer, not all jobs are pensionable.

Self-development   A number of charities have staff development programmes, and will certainly encourage you to get extra qualifications since this will enable the organisation to be run more efficiently.

Self-expression There are a number of arts based charities with opportunities to use one's artistic talents. Creativity is also needed on the fundraising front and a good personality can be important when dealing with both clients and donors.

Social relevance Charities and voluntary organisations are high on the social relevance scale, and often do work that tends to get overlooked by the public and private sectors.

Status You probably won't become famous through working for a charity, but normally people working in the voluntary sector enjoy a good deal of respect for what they do.

Variety This will depend very much on the size of the charity you are working for. If you are working in a small team you have to deploy a much greater range of skills and have to deal with a range of situations.

WHAT KIND OF ORGANISATION WOULD SUIT YOU?

No two charities are the same. Each one has a particular ethos and even if they are operating within the same sector, they may differ in aims and approach. Some may be young, thrusting and dynamic; others may be rather more staid and bureaucratic; some may focus particularly on fundraising in order to finance of the work of other organisations; others will place more emphasis of delivery of services. In some volunteers play a major role; others are largely dependent on professionals.

You may find there is a considerable difference between how a large charity and a small to medium charity is run. Let's have a look at some of the possible differences from the staff point of view.

Working for a large organisation: the pros and cons
Pros

- Can offer a good career with prospects

- Has secure funding, so jobs are safe

- Is well-established and prestigious

- Offers opportunities for staff development

- Employees have a chance to move to other jobs within the organisation.

Cons

- It might be impersonal and bureaucratic

- You may feel like a cog in a wheel

- There could be little opportunity to use your initiative

- Greater competition for vacancies means jobs are harder to get.

Working for a small to medium-sized organisation: the pros and cons
Pros

- You are involved in a greater range of tasks

- You get more chance to use your initiative

- You are more closely involved in any decision making

- There is a greater sense of teamwork

- There may be fewer applicants for vacancies, making it easier to get a job.

Cons

● Pay may be below average

● Your job may not be secure because of funding uncertainties

● There may be limited scope for promotion or development

● The organisation may suffer from a lack of clear direction

● You may find yourself overwhelmed by your responsibilities.

There is no substitute for doing in-depth research into the charities that appeal to you, and there are plenty of sources of information available. Your local reference library will probably stock at least one of these books:

Charity Choice: The Encyclopaedia of Charities
This contains entries for some 8000 voluntary organisations and provides their contact addresses, telephone numbers and websites. Some descriptions are more detailed than others. There are separate volumes for Scotland and Northern Ireland. This information is also available on the internet (www.charitychoice.co.uk).

The Major Charities: An Independent Guide, Luke Herbert and Kathryn Becker
Although it may not list as many charities, it provides extensive details on 165 major charities, including the proportion of their income devoted to fundraising. In addition, there are 30 group entries (ranging from hospices to cancer care charities) plus a list the top 500 fundraising charities.

Voluntary Agencies Directory (NCVO)
This lists 2000 voluntary organisations and charities with a description of each one and contact details.

There are also a number of websites, such as Guidestar UK (www.guidestar.org.uk) and Charities Direct (www.charitiesdirect.com), which provide information on different charities. And do not ignore the websites of the individual charities themselves, some of which are very informative indeed.

Most publish annual reports that are freely available and give useful insights into the aims of the charity and their plans for the future. Don't overlook specialist periodicals, such as *VS* and *Third Sector* which often feature profiles of different voluntary organisations. Some of the larger reference libraries may well stock these periodicals.

ARE YOU SUITED TO THIS TYPE OF WORK?

Some people know from the start what kind of career they want to follow and show great determination to get it. Others take time to find their niche and may tackle a number of different jobs before they get settled. While you can rely to a certain extent on what you are told about a particular organisation, there is no substitute for first hand experience within it.

There are people who have tremendous self-confidence in their abilities and are prepared to apply for any job they fancy. On the other hand there are those who are deterred from applying because they feel they have neither qualifications nor experience in charity work.

Professional qualifications are a definite asset for certain jobs, such as marketing, fundraising, social work and counselling, and will give you the edge over rival applicants. But other jobs may require few, if any, formal qualifications at all; just the ability to be practical, flexible and able to handle people. The snag is that many charities can find volunteers to do this kind of work.

You should not discount the importance of transferable skills – portable skills that have relevance to virtually any job you undertake. Look at the following questions and tick those of which you have experience.

☐ Have you ever been the treasurer of a club? If so you will have experience of handling money and making financial decisions

☐ Have you every worked in a shop? If so you will have acquired customer care skills

☐ Have you ever had to explain to someone how a particular gadget (eg a mobile phone) works? If so you have analytical and communication skills

☐ Have you ever had to look after young people (eg as a Scout or Guide leader)? If so, you will have gained leadership skills

☐ Have you ever done a First Aid course with the St John Ambulance or Red Cross? These are practical skills that not every job applicant has

☐ Can you drive? The ability to drive can count very much in your favour particularly in a job that involves a lot of visiting

☐ Have you ever had to make a presentation (eg at school or college)? Presentational skills are important in the voluntary sector

☐ Have you experience of using computers for word processing and looking things up on the internet? Good IT skills will stand you in good stead in most walks of life

☐ Have you ever edited a newsletter or written articles for a magazine or newspaper? Good verbal skills can be most useful in the voluntary sector

☐ Have you ever organised a trip for a group of people or an event? Success in these areas will demonstrate organisational ability.

Concentrate on the questions that you marked with a tick. It is worthwhile making a note of the skills that you have, because one day you will need to sell yourself and your skills to prospective employers. It is no use expecting them to tease out your abilities from the application form you submit; you have to be aware of what you can offer and bring them out forcefully in your application, ideally backed with solid evidence.

If your work experience has been outside the voluntary sector, you should not regard this as a handicap. Most charities welcome people who have worked in commerce or government since they often have much needed professional skills which will benefit the charity. A friendly personality, reliability and the ability to work as part of a team are important assets, too.

HOW TO ACQUIRE THE NECESSARY SKILLS

The voluntary sector is becoming increasingly attractive to jobseekers these days and the competition for jobs means that employers are becoming more demanding. One charity recruitment agency specifies that applicants for jobs should have:

- At least six months' experience in the job you are applying for

- At least one year's work experience

- A good level of education

- Training relevant to the position

- Proven commitment to the charity sector through paid experience or volunteering.

This may seem a very tall order, and you may well wonder how on earth you get started in your chosen career. If you find your list of skills is disappointingly short, you should endeavour to get extra experience, perhaps by volunteering (see Case Study 4). Most charities are keen to recruit volunteers, whether on a regular or a one-off basis. If you are unable to make a long-term commitment, it doesn't really matter. Such organisations welcome short-term help at holiday times when some of their regular volunteers are away. There is no age barrier to volunteering; volunteers of all ages can be considered. Although professional qualifications are a definite asset for certain jobs, such as marketing, fundraising, social work and counselling, other jobs may require few, if any; just the ability to be practical, flexible and able to handle people. The charity sector is one place where it is still possible to start at the bottom and work your way to the top, though soon this may no longer be the case.

Here is a selection of tasks you could perform as a volunteer which could provide you with some very worthwhile experience:

- Manning telephone support lines (eg the Samaritans)

- Taking round meals on wheels (eg WRVS)

- Manning an information desk at your local hospital (eg Hospital League of Friends)

- Befriending vulnerable people (eg Victim Support)

- Helping to run activities for young people (eg youth club)

- Teaching handicapped people reading and other skills (eg Scope)

- Sending out appeals for funds (various charities)

- Doing a street collection (various charities)

- Organising a fundraising event, such as a fete or a sponsored race

- Looking after old or disabled people under supervision in a day care centre

- Helping out at an animal shelter or clinic

- Gardening and home maintenance for the elderly and handicapped

- Acting as a presenter or providing technical help for a hospital radio station.

You can also gain useful experience through joining the committee of your local film society, college union, football club, old people's club, local arts association or civic amenities society, for instance, which will give you an invaluable insight into how not for profit organisations are run and the challenges they face.

An increasing number of people take a gap year and spend part of it involved in worthwhile work projects both at home and abroad; and that is an idea worth considering. Gap years used to be mainly the preserve of young people between school and university, but today the 25–35 year old age group comprise the fastest growing sector of the gap year market. Gap years on useful projects not only enable you to develop new skills, they also broaden your horizons.

Among the organisations which offer such an experience abroad are:

- BUNAC

- Frontier

- GAP Challenge

- i to i International Projects

- Oasis Trust

- Raleigh International

- Teaching & Projects Abroad

- Travellers

- VSO.

(For a more comprehensive list of gap year opportunities please refer to *You Want To Work Where?!* (Trotman, 2003)

There are also organisations which offer a chance to do volunteer work away from home in the UK, notably Community Service Volunteers. CSV have a special young volunteer programme for people aged 16–35 which often involves working with the elderly, children and the disabled.

For more mature people with extensive management experience VSO offers short-term 'troubleshooting' assignments. REACH fulfils a similar function in the UK.

Incidentally, these organisations also have paid staff to run the organisations and look after the needs of the volunteers and there are many examples of people who have moved on from being a volunteer to assume a supervisory role in a particular organisation.

HOW TO BECOME INVOLVED AS A VOLUNTEER

There are a number of ways into volunteering.

● You may know of a local charity that is on the lookout for volunteers.

● You could contact your local volunteer centre (these are sometimes called Centres for Voluntary Action) which you will find in your local telephone directory. Many have their own websites or publicise their requirements in local newspapers.

● You could try the national volunteering database by logging on to www.do-it.org.uk. You simply enter your postcode and will get a list of vacancies available in your area. Alternatively you could contact Volunteering England (www.volunteering.org.uk).

● You could simply ask around. With over 13 million people doing volunteer work at least once a month in the UK, the chances are that you already know quite a few people who do volunteer work in their spare time. Tell them you're interested in volunteering and would like to give it a whirl.

● You may see an appeal for volunteers in a newspaper, especially a local newspaper either in a news report or in an advertisement. The *Guardian* advertises for volunteers in its *Society Guardian* on Wednesdays. A recent issue had requests for volunteer fundraisers, animal care helpers, volunteer counsellors, volunteer administrators for a therapy centre, volunteer mentors for young people and telephone counsellors.

FINDING OUT MORE ABOUT THE VOLUNTARY SECTOR

Some volunteer centres offer training to give people who are thinking of volunteering an insight into what is involved. However, if you are considering making a career in this sector the 'Working for a Charity' training courses run by the National Council for Voluntary Organisations (NCVO) are well worth looking at. These courses offer information and advice for people from many different backgrounds: career changers, young people at the start of their careers and people who want to re-enter the world of work after an absence.

'Working for a Charity' currently offers three kinds of courses, which are described below.

INTRODUCTORY PROGRAMME
This takes place in two evening sessions held in Central London, each of which lasts approximately two hours. As its title implies, it serves as a brief introduction to the voluntary sector and is divided into two parts:

● Part 1 describes the shape of the voluntary sector and job opportunities within it

● Part 2 covers the role of fundraising in the voluntary sector.

FOUNDATION COURSE
This course is intended for people seeking a career in the voluntary sector and combines seven days of seminars with a 20 day placement in a host charity. It is particularly useful for people looking for their first paid job in the voluntary sector. The course describes the shape of the voluntary sector and job opportunities within it.

The programme consists of seven full-day seminars and workshops spread over several weeks and runs concurrently with a placement. The combination of theory and group work on the training days and the placement is intended to help each individual gain further insights into how their skills might be usefully applied and where they might best fit in the sector. The overall programme can be completed within a period of 8–12 weeks with an average commitment of two or three days each week.

Among the topics covered by the course are:

● Understanding the voluntary sector

● Jobs in the voluntary sector

● Marketing and public relations in the voluntary sector

● Developing a fundraising strategy

● Charitable trust funding and company giving

● Financial management, governance and the role of volunteers

● Equal opportunities, successful interviews, a springboard for the future.

A fee is payable for the course but a limited number of Foundation course bursaries are available to cover up to 50% of the cost.

THREE DAY EXECUTIVE PROGRAMME

This three day intensive course is for people in full-time employment who wish to explore opportunities in the voluntary sector with minimal disruption to their current job. It would also be useful for anyone who has recently been appointed to a position of responsibility within the sector, whether paid or unpaid, who wishes to gain a further understanding of key issues they are likely to face.

WHAT CAN YOU OFFER?

It is now time to look at yourself and decide what you have to offer an employer in the voluntary sector. If you have recently completed full-time education, you may see yourself in terms of the subjects you have studied and the qualifications you have gained. Of course, these are important, but they should not overshadow the other skills you have picked up along the way, which may be of even greater relevance to the job you eventually find than your dissertation on Beowulf or research into particle physics. That is why it is important to look at yourself and decide what you have to offer before plunging into the process of job applications. If you don't know what you can do, you are not going to sell yourself very effectively to an interviewing panel.

To understand the process let us take an imaginary person whom we will call Joanna Jolliman. Joanna is just about to graduate in Social Studies and she is interested in a voluntary sector job in animal welfare or working with the disadvantaged. She wonders whether her degree will be sufficient to land her the job she wants.

It is certainly in the right sort of discipline. Other recommended fields of study for the charity sector are:

- Business studies

- Community development

- Economics

- Finance and accountancy

- Law

- Marketing

- PR

- Social policy and development

- Sociology

- Voluntary sector management.

However, the subject of the degree or diploma may not be the overriding influence on the selector's decision, unless they are recruiting for a specialist post (such as a legal adviser or finance director). Personality, motivation, adaptability and other personal attributes, for which there are no formal qualifications, are often judged more important.

Joanna should not overlook the fact that studying for a degree not only gave her subject knowledge, it enabled her to acquire other skills. For instance:

● She had to do research for her dissertation

● She had to analyse the facts she found and draw conclusions from them

● She had to present her findings to her tutor and justify them to him

● She also had to interview people involved in various social projects.

So altogether she has research skills, analytical skills, presentational skills and interviewing skills, all of which could be assets if she got a job in the charity sector. And there may well be other skills that she has acquired during her studies.

However, this experience may seem insignificant if she is up against stiff competition for a job. Other applicants may be from prestigious universities and have gained plenty of experience along the way. They will surely cut more impressive figures than Joanna.

This may be so, but Joanna needs to recall the other things she has done which were not related to her degree course at all. She is not a dull girl whose life was all work and no play. She did other things in her spare time.

● She did a First Aid course when she was at school

● She joined the university drama club and became its secretary

- She organised social events at her hall of residence

- She did regular counselling sessions at the local office of the Samaritans

- She took up lacrosse and became the captain of the university women's team

- She wrote articles for the college newspaper and became its features editor

- She ran a campaign for the winning candidate in the Student Union presidential election.

As a result of her extracurricular activities Joanna acquired experience of First Aid, committee work (including the writing of minutes), organisational skills, counselling skills, leadership skills and verbal ability. Her campaigning flair would be invaluable to her chosen charity's fundraising team. With this experience she will not have to acquire these skills from scratch if she lands a job with a voluntary organisation.

Joanna is also bothered by the fact that she will be up against people with full-time jobs who have plenty of professional work experience. But if she thinks carefully she has actually had a number of jobs during her summer vacations and in her first year as an undergraduate she had a part-time job working in a local pub. If she lists them on a piece of paper she will be able to analyse what useful skills or experience she has gained from these.

- Last summer she went abroad and taught English at a summer camp for disadvantaged children in Romania

- The previous summer she worked for a department store in her home town

- For her first year at university she worked at a pub as a waitress and behind the bar

- During the summer between school and university she worked at an animal refuge.

This is all very convincing evidence of Joanna's abilities. She has teaching skills and, experience of different cultures (an asset if she eventually wishes to join an international charity). Her experience of retailing would prove attractive to a charity with a trading arm (charity shops). She has worked in the hospitality sector and presumably acquired good customer care skills. And her background in an animal sanctuary would be a good selling point if she decides to go after a job in an animal charity.

So what skills has Joanna got to offer? Here is a summary of them:

- Research skills

- Analytical ability

- Presentation skills

- Interviewing skills

- First Aid skills

- Secretarial skills

- Committee experience

- Organising skills

- Counselling skills

- Leadership skills

- Verbal ability

- Campaigning skills

- Teaching experience

- Cultural awareness

- Retail experience

- Customer care skills

- Hospitality skills

- Animal welfare experience.

If you examine job vacancy advertisements in the voluntary sector you will find that many of these skills feature in the job description. What Joanna needs to do is to list these skills and how she acquired them and have the list at her side for reference when she makes a job application. Every job seeker should take note and follow her example.

After reading this account, some readers may believe that Joanna is more like Superwoman than a real person. However, as mentioned at the start, she is a figment of the imagination, designed to encourage people – of any age – to look closely at themselves and consider the whole range of skills they could offer to organisations in this sector. You have to work out what you have to offer and then present yourself convincingly drawing attention to your assets. If you don't do either of these things how on earth are you going to persuade a potential employer to give you a job?

Now let's consider how Joanna's CV might look.

SAMPLE CV

JOANNA JOLLIMAN

Home address	**Correspondence address**
	(until 15 June)
20 Acacia Avenue,	Pineview Hall,
Oakleigh,	Elmstead,
Willowshire	Aldershire
WW3 7WW	AA9 BB2
Tel. 01999 543211	Tel. 011111 222222 ext. 33

Mobile: 0999 876543   **Email:** joanna@joannajolliman.net.
Date of birth: 31 December 1987

EDUCATION
1997–2002   Larch Rise School, Oakleigh
2002–2004   Oakleigh Sixth Form College
2004–2007   Elmstead University

QUALIFICATIONS
2000   A Level: Biology (B), Chemistry (C), Geography (C),
       Business Studies (A)
1998   GCSE: History (A), English Language (B), Biology
       (B),Geography (B), Mathematics (C), Chemistry (C),
       Spanish (C)

I am currently studying for a BA in Social Studies, and will
take my Finals in the summer.

WORK EXPERIENCE
2006   Summer job with **Romania Rescue** teaching English at
a summer camp for disadvantaged children in Romania at
which I also arranged recreational activities.

2005   **Sales Assistant** (temporary summer job), Finegoods
Department Store. I worked in the children's clothing
department and deputised for the head of the department
when she went on holiday.

2004–2005   **Waitress and Bartender** (PT), The Pig and Whistle, Elmstead. I worked for six months at this establishment and supervised the bar on the Duty Manager's night off.

2004   **Animal Welfare Assistant,** Animal Refuge, Oakleigh. This was a six week summer job during which I was responsible for feeding and caring for the animals and assisting the vet in treatments and inspections.

INTERESTS
Drama: I was Secretary of the Drama Club from 2005–2007
Lacrosse: I was captain of the University Women's Lacrosse Team 2006–2007
Creative Writing: I am currently features editor of the *Elmstead University Echo.*

OTHER INFORMATION
I possess a clean driving licence and a First Aid Certificate from the St John Ambulance. I have also been a telephone counsellor with the Samaritans. I shall be free to take up an appointment from July onwards.

Points to note:

- Joanna offers plenty of contact details including where she will be when.

- She includes examinations passed at school. More mature candidates with plenty of work experience would not need to go in such detail but put more emphasis on post-school qualifications.

- Although she has not held any permanent posts she mentions temporary and part-time jobs she has done and gives a brief description of what the work entailed.

- She uses the 'Interests' section to draw attention to her talents in these fields. The fact that she played a leading role in *The*

Importance of Being Earnest will cut less ice with the selectors than her secretarial responsibilities in the drama club.

- She mentions other skills, such as driving and counselling, both of which could be of relevance to a job in the voluntary sector.

- She informs the recipient of the CV as to when she will be available to take up any job.

CHAPTER 4

The next stage

Once you have decided you want to work in this sector, you need to look for a job. There are various ways of doing this

RESPONDING TO A JOB ADVERTISEMENT

If you are looking for work in your particular area, have a look through the job advertisements in your local newspaper. If you are prepared to go further afield you could look in the national press, especially:

- *Guardian*: Monday for PR and marketing, Tuesday for educational jobs, Wednesday for general charity jobs and Saturday for all areas

- *Independent:* Monday for media jobs, Thursday for general charity jobs, Sunday for management jobs

- *The Times:* Thursday

- *Daily Telegraph:* Thursday

- *The Sunday Times*

- *Observer*

You could also look in specialist periodicals that serve the charity sector

● *Professional Fundraising*

● *Third Sector*

● *VS Magazine*

● *Social Caringe*

● *NFP Jobs* (This is an on-line newsletter: http://nfpjobs.netxtra.net)

If you have a particular specialism, such as accountancy or marketing, you will also find the voluntary sector often advertises more specialist posts in the relevant professional or trade journals (eg *Accountancy Age, Marketing Week, Campaign*).

The advantage of applying for an advertised vacancy is that you know that there is a job available and it might be with a charity you may not have considered. The disadvantage is that the vacancy may attract a large number of applicants against whom you will have to compete.

Tips.

1. Make sure you read the details of the advertisement carefully to work out what skills the organisation is looking for.
2. Note the deadline for applications. If the deadline is close consider faxing or emailing your application unless you are specifically told to submit your application by post.
3. Make a note of the contact details and any reference number to make sure your communication does not go astray and file away the ad for future reference.
4. Be clear what you have to do. Do you have to send off for an application form or supply them with your CV?

Look at the instructions in the job advertisement. Here are some recent examples

● To apply, please send your CV and a covering letter of application demonstrating your relevant skills and expertise in relation to the job description and person specification.

● For an application pack please visit our website or contact us on (telephone number).

● Visit our website to complete an on-line application form or telephone our HR Office for an application form by post. Do not send a CV.

APPROACHING A CHARITY DIRECT

This approach, known as the speculative approach, involves contacting a charity (or a number of charities) and telling them what skills and experience you can offer and the type of job you are after. The traditional way of applying direct involves sending an eye-catching letter backed up by a CV or a well presented email message. Generally speaking, telephoning a charity is less productive, since the staff are normally too busy to have time to deal with a speculative caller. However, it is a perfectly legitimate means of finding out to whom you should send your application.

The advantage of this method is that you may find out about a vacancy before it is advertised. The disadvantage is that it could be rather a hit and miss affair, rather like the cold calling of a double-glazing salesman. However, this approach works perfectly well if you are applying to be a volunteer.

Tips

1. Make sure you know something about the charity in question before you contact anybody. Have a look at its website beforehand and look for stories in the charity press about charities that are planning to expand.
2. It is more impressive if you can write to somebody with a name rather than just address your correspondence to the personnel manager.
3. Don't be vague. Mention experience or qualifications you have which would be of definite interest to the organisation.
4. If the charity doesn't have a job to offer, thank them courteously for their trouble and ask if they would like to keep your details on file.

SPECIMEN LETTER FOR SPECULATIVE APPLICATION

20 Wuthering Heights
Wetherby
Yorks YO76 1XX
Tel: 01234 567890

28 March 200X

Mr Duncan Le Page,
Director,
Action Everything,
Fishpond Lane,
London W29 5SS

Dear Mr Le Page,

I am currently seeking employment in the voluntary sector and having read about your charity on your excellent website I am keen to join it.

I am currently working for a private sector company, having graduated in Business Studies from Archbishop's College two years ago. A lot of my spare time, however, is spent doing voluntary work which I have found particularly challenging and enjoyable. As a result I now want to work in the voluntary sector on a full-time basis.

I am aware that working for a charity requires professionalism of a high order and I can assure you that I well motivated, well organised and ready to take the initiative. My current employers have frequently complimented me for my meticulous work and ability to meet difficult deadlines.

I first started doing charity work when I was at school when I helped at a school for the disabled. I managed a charity shop for the British Heart Foundation one summer, was a Guide leader, and have recently been working with teenage drug addicts. I am also honorary treasurer of the Wetherby Performing Arts Association.

I would be very glad to visit you at a mutually convenient time to discuss how I could deploy my talents for the benefit of your organisation.

You can contact me on the telephone number above or email me at rmayhew@britnet.com.

Yours sincerely,

Rita Mayhew

Question: How will Mr Le Page react to this speculative letter and will he offer Rita a job if he has one?

Mr Le Page should be fairly impressed by this letter. It is direct and to the point and Rita shows enthusiasm for the charity: she must be enthusiastic if she has looked at its website. And she has used some very positive vocabulary when describing her skills (well motivated, well organised, initiative, meticulous). But rather than dwelling on the work she does in the firm for which she works, she emphasises her voluntary activities, which are likely to be of greater interest to Mr Le Page. She manages to get her foot in the door by offering to meet him, and leaves clear directions as to how she can be contacted. Mr Le Page's curiosity is likely to be roused and he will want to see her to see if she is as good as she sounds.

REGISTERING WITH A RECRUITMENT AGENCY

A number of charities outsource their recruitment to recruitment agencies, which either advertise a particular post or consult their database of candidates. Some of them specialise in recruiting for middle and senior management jobs or for overseas development organisations, but there are no hard and fast rules.

There has been a considerable upsurge in the number of agencies that specialise in recruitment for the voluntary and not for profit sectors. They include:

- Aquilas

- Charity Action Recruitment

- Charity Careers

- Charity Connections

- CF Appointments

- Charity People

- Charity Recruitment

- Charity Futures

- Eden Brown

- Execucare

- Flow Caritas

- Harris Hill

- Jobs in Charities

- Kage Partnership

- Lifeline Personnel

- Morgan Hunt

- NfP Resourcing

- Oxford Human Resource Consultants

- ProspectUs

- The Principle Partnership.

You will find their addresses and websites in the Resources chapter.

The advantage of using agencies is that a single agency will recruit for a number of charities, not just one, which will increase your chances of finding a job which suits you. Another is that if you impress the agency it may be willing to help identify the jobs and organisations to which you would seem best suited. The drawback is that not all voluntary organisations use agencies, preferring to use their own resources.

Tips

1. Don't just try one recruitment agency, otherwise you will be limiting your options.

2. Mention that you are quite happy to meet one of the recruitment consultants to discuss job possibilities in the voluntary sector.
3. If someone agrees to see you, treat this as practice for a real job interview and look your best. If you can't impress the consultant he is unlikely to recommend you to any of his clients.
4. Be prepared to ask some pertinent questions, eg about the current recruitment requirements of particular charities.

SEARCHING ON THE INTERNET

If you have access to the internet – and most people have these days – you will be able to find out what vacancies are available. You can do this by accessing the website of different charities and organisations and turning to their recruitment pages. In this way you can read up about the charity concerned and find out if they have any jobs which would suit you.

The website of recruitment agencies work in a similar way, except that they usually have many more vacancies on offer. Some sites (such as the Jobs in Charities one) can even conduct a job search for you. You simply key in:

● The kind of job you are looking for; the categories will usually be similar to the categories shown in Chapter 3

● The type of charity voluntary organisation you would like to work for

● The location where you would prefer to work.

Don't expect to find the job you want at the first attempt. If you restrict your options to a particular type of job and a particular location nothing may come up on then screen. If you are prepared to specify more than one position and several locations you may have more success.

Some websites have a facility whereby you can apply for a job on-line. If you have the option to download the form and send it by snail mail, this might be preferable, as you will be able to complete it at your leisure.

Tips

1. Bear in mind that some of the information on the website may be out of date, including the job details.
2. Most organisations will expect you to submit your application on hard copy.
3. If you decide to fill in the application form on-line, be very careful and take your time. If you make lots of typographical errors you are less likely to impress the selectors.
4. Make sure you check your inbox regularly, as you may be asked to go for an interview at short notice.

ATTENDING A JOBS FAIR

Jobs fairs are another way of finding a job. They usually take place at exhibition centres and their focus may be on general employment, school leavers or newly qualified graduates. A number of university careers offices arrange such events, one of the biggest being the London Graduate Recruitment Fair which can attract up to half a million people. There are also local recruitment fairs, often organised in conjunction with local newspapers.

Some of them are directed at the particular sectors, such as the not for profit sector and it would be worthwhile contacting the organisers of these events to enquire when and where they are due to be held. London and Manchester are popular venues and a number of these take place in the autumn.

The main organisers are:

● Directory of Social Change: Charity Fair

● Forum 3

● Society Guardian Live.

The advantage of attending recruitment fairs is that you get a chance to speak freely to people who are in the business of recruiting staff and you will be able to find out about a number of organisations in a short time without any obligation on your part.

The disadvantage is that only a limited number of organisations may be represented and they may not be the particular ones that you are interested in.

Tips

1. Take a notebook with you and note down the main points of each discussion you have.
2. Ask for brochures on the organisations which interest you and file them away carefully.
3. Ask for contacts in the organisation and make a note of the person you have been talking to.
4. Dress reasonably smartly. Although this isn't an interview, first impressions do count.

NETWORKING

In the distant past people tended to rely on friends and relations to find them jobs. Although this was branded as nepotism, it worked, and you should not hesitate to make use of what contacts you have, especially if you know people who are working in the voluntary sector. Careers advisory centres and Connexions staff are also useful sources of information and can certainly steer you in the right direction.

Tips

1. Have a CV with you just in case your contact(s) would like to see it.
2. Don't be pushy and expect your contact(s) to get you a job as matter of course.
3. Keep your contact(s) informed as to your job hunting progress.
4. Don't expect your contact(s) to move heaven and earth to help you. It may be that they are in no position to assist.

APPLYING FOR THE JOB

Although the internet is revolutionising communications these days the usual way of submitting your application for a job you have seen advertised remains by post. It will normally consist of two or three items, namely:

- A covering letter

- Your CV and/or

- Your application form.

These items need to be neatly presented on A4 paper (white or tinted) of at least 80 gsm thickness and sent off either in an A5 or A4 size envelope by first class post. Sending it second class might suggest that you are less than enthusiastic about the job or just plain stingy.

Let us look at these three items in turn.

THE COVERING LETTER

There is some debate as to whether selectors take much notice of candidate's letters. The answer is that some do and some don't, preferring to immerse themselves in the details of the CV or application form. The voluntary sector, however, might be particularly interested in your letter writing abilities, as writing letters may well be a part of the job. Communication skills will almost certainly be.

So it would be sensible to pay attention to your letter. Unless the advertisement specifically asks for a handwritten letter – some organisations employ graphologists who claim to interpret a person's character from their handwriting – you should type it, particularly if your handwriting is illegible or a sight for sore eyes. Also you should use A4 paper like your CV.

QUIZ
Imagine you are shortlisting candidates for a job interview.
Which one of these would you select on the strength of the
covering letter and why?

A

> 5 Juniper Square
> Dalkeith
> DK1 2GH
>
> 20 June 200X

Human Resource Manager
Caithness Voluntary Services Council

Dear Sir,

With reference to your advertisement for a volunteer co-
ordinator at the Robert Bruce Volunteer Centre. I enclose a
copy of my CV and a completed application form.

I await further instructions.

Yours truly,

John Green

_____

B

> 20 Honeysuckle Terrace
> Durham
> NE90 1YY
> Tel: 01987 654321
>
> 20th June 200X

Human Resource Manager
Caithness Voluntary Services Council
1 Culloden Place
Caithness

Dear Sir

I wish to be considered for the post of volunteer director with your organisation.

As you will see from my CV, I have a degree in Food Science from Newcastle University and have been interested in the voluntary sector for the past three years.

I hope you will consider me for the job.

Regards,

Cathy Brown

_____

c

12 River View
Ayr
AY8 4SD

20.5.0X

Mr Jeremy Orange
Human Resource Manager
Caithness Voluntary Services Council
1 Culloden Place
Caithness CN12 0GH

Dear Mr Orange,

Thank you so much for sending me details of the volunteer director vacancy at the Robert Bruce Volunteer Centre. Having read the information with great interest I am more convinced than ever that this is the job for me.

I am a self-starter who relishes an opportunity to take the initiative and motivate others to give of their best. This is in some measure due to the leadership skills course I attended last year and my involvement with people from all walks of life.

I should like to highlight the fact that while at university I ran a summer camp for disadvantaged children from Bosnia and have been on the management committee of my local youth council for the past 18 months.

I look forward to meeting you to learn more about the work of the Centre and the challenges of the job. If you are unable to contact me you can leave a message on my answerphone or email me at rviolet@hairnet.co.uk.

Yours sincerely,

Richard Violet

Comments on covering letters

John Green's letter is terse. It is a covering letter and nothing more than that, and is clearly written in haste because he has left out the address of the organisation and doesn't even credit the HR Manager with a name.

Cathy's is better. She gives information about her degree course but, frankly, the subject she studied is irrelevant to the job. Also she furnishes little proof of her involvement with the voluntary sector. The final sentence is a little weak as she is unsure of herself.

Richard engages with the HR Manager from the start. He even mentions him by name!

He expresses enthusiasm for the job, which he clearly wants. He describes his outlook on life – you could even call it his 'managerial style' – and he supports these statements with some evidence. He ends on a positive note: he is sure that he is going to be invited for an interview and he makes sure he

> doesn't miss the summons by giving precise contact instructions. Richard's letter will carry most weight with the type of selector who reads forwarding letters. You may consider it a bit over the top, but it conveys a positive impression and is just about the right length for a letter of this kind. Two or three page letters are likely to get ignored.

EVALUATING YOUR CV

We discussed CVs in the last chapter. Have you written your CV yet? If not get down to this task right away using Joanna Jolliman's as your model. With luck you will be able to improve on her effort.

Now look at it carefully.

- Are there ways that you could tailor it to the job for which you are applying?

- Are there points not relevant to the job which could be omitted?

- Have you included all your relevant skills, not just your qualifications?

- Have you described what your past employment entailed?

- Is it neatly and clearly laid out?

- Have you shown it to anyone for comment?

- Are you expected to submit a CV?

This latter question may seem strange, but some advertisements specify that they do not want CVs. Selectors prefer to have the information set out in a standardised manner on one of their own application forms.

COMPLETING THE APPLICATION FORM

While some people have no difficulty in typing in the details on application forms it can be a fiddly business, and you may find it is much easier to write in the details. Do this slowly and carefully using capital letters where specified and printing other details. (With on-line application forms you have to type in the information.)

Appearances count, and if your application form looks like a battlefield because of the many deletions and corrections, you will not make a good impression on the selectors. For this reason it makes sense to photocopy the form and practise on that before completing the master-copy.

There is no need to fill in everything on the form. If a particular item does not apply to you write 'Not Applicable' or 'N/A'. However, in no circumstances should you put a line through the form in a fit of pique and write the words 'Refer to CV'. If you find you have insufficient space, you could continue on the back of the form or note down the extra details on a sheet of blank paper.

There is a tendency for application forms to leave spaces in which you have to describe yourself and your aspirations. Make sure you express yourself accurately and grammatically and try to emphasis your strong points without sounding boastful.

Most application forms ask you to nominate referees. While an academic reference or a former employer's reference is fine, if there is someone who has supervised you or knows of your voluntary efforts, or a responsible person who has known you for some time, he or she would be the ideal person to write a reference.

SAMPLE APPLICATION FORM

POST APPLIED FOR _____

SURNAME _____ FIRST NAMES _____

ADDRESS _____

_____

_____

TELEPHONE NUMBER _____

EMAIL ADDRESS _____

SEX _____ NATIONALITY _____

DATE OF BIRTH _____ PLACE OF BIRTH _____

MARITAL STATUS _____

EDUCATION

Dates	Institution	Qualifications achieved

EMPLOYMENT HISTORY

Dates	Employer's name & address	Title & responsibilities

MEMBERSHIP OF PROFESSIONAL ASSOCIATIONS

_____

_____

ADDITIONAL TRAINING COURSES ATTENDED

_____

_____

HOBBIES, SPORTS & OTHER INTERESTS

_____

_____

DO YOU HOLD A FULL CURRENT DRIVING LICENCE? _____

HAVE YOU SUFFERED ANY SERIOUS ILLNESSES DURING THE PAST
FIVE YEARS? _____

IF SO GIVE DETAILS

_____

DO YOU HAVE ANY CONVICTIONS OTHER THAN FOR MINOR
OFFENCES? _____

IF SO GIVE DETAILS.

_____

SUPPLY THE NAMES AND ADDRESSES OF THREE PEOPLE WHO CAN
COMMENT ON YOUR SUITABILITY FOR THE POST

_____

_____

_____

EXPLAIN BRIEFLY WHY YOU WISH TO BE CONSIDERED FOR THIS
POST AND WHAT EXPERTISE YOU COULD BRING TO IT

_____

_____

_____

GIVE DETAILS OF VOLUNTARY WORK YOU HAVE DONE

_____

_____

_____

GIVE DETAILS OF ANY INTERESTS, ACTIVITIES OR OTHER
INFORMATION WHICH YOU CONSIDER RELEVANT TO YOUR
APPLICATION

_____

_____

_____

I AFFIRM THAT TO THE BEST OF MY KNOWLEDGE THE
INFORMATION GIVEN ABOVE IS CORRECT.

SIGNED _____
DATE _____

EXERCISE

Joanna Jolliman has decided to apply for the post of fundraising assistant with the charity Help the Disadvantaged. Using the information you have about her on pages 56 to 60 complete the form for her with the intention of making her application stand out.

Joanna's application form: comments and suggestions

● **Additional training courses attended**　She needs to mention her First Aid Course. Most offices like to have a First Aider they can call upon in an emergency.

● **Hobbies, sports & other interests**　Her interest in lacrosse, drama and creative writing need to be stated, with a description of each, if there is sufficient room.

● **Do you hold a full current driving licence?**　This could be useful if she has to go off to meet potential donors.

● **Have you suffered any serious illnesses during the past five years?**　Hopefully she hasn't. A serious illness is one that puts you out of action for a substantial period of time. A week off with a cold doesn't qualify. However if she has been in hospital for an operation recently, this should be mentioned.

● **Do you have any convictions other than for minor offences?**　Probably not. A parking fine or failure to pay one's TV licence are not major offences.

● **Supply the names and addresses of three people who can comment on your suitability for the post**　Ideally she needs at least one person who can comment on her work: the duty manager at the pub, the department manager at Finegoods or even better her supervisor at Romania Rescue. Her tutor at Elmstead University should provide and academic reference and maybe there is someone in her hometown who has known her for several years who can provide a personal reference.

● **Explain briefly why you wish to be considered for this post and what expertise you could bring to it**   She should mention her interest in the charity sector stimulated by her summer job with Romania Rescue, her work with the Samaritans and perhaps the course in which she will shortly be graduating. As for expertise in fundraising, she has analytical and presentational skills as a result of her course (useful for talking to potential donors), she can write and edit (and would presumably be able to put together a newsletter for supporters), she has retail experience (which means she can contribute her experience to the charity's trading arm, if it has one), she has experience of running a successful campaign (for the presidential election) and she has experience of committee work (the drama club).

● **Give details of voluntary work you have done** Counselling with the Samaritans is a good start. If she has done any street or door to door collections for charity this is also worth mentioning.

● **Give details of any interests, activities or other information which you consider relevant to your application**   It might be sensible to emphasise her international experience in Romania, since that will suggest she is flexible and open-minded. Her experience in the hospitality industry might be of interest if the charity has fundraising receptions and will certainly show that she is used to dealing with people of all types.

The point of this exercise is to show how you should draw on all aspects of your experience, analyse which ones are of relevance to the position applied for and present the information convincingly.

PREPARING FOR THE INTERVIEW

If you are invited to an interview it is time to pat yourself on the back. Some jobs attract hundreds of applicants and in such circumstances getting to this stage is no mean feat. But you cannot afford to be complacent, since the job is not yet in the bag. There is another hurdle to be overcome and you need to prepare for it in earnest.

You must research the organisation thoroughly. In the days of the internet there is absolutely no excuse for turning up before a board of selectors blissfully ignorant on the aims and activities of the organisation you are hoping to work for, even if you are merely applying to become the office boy or a Girl Friday.

Some organisations will send you a detailed job description so that you will know exactly what the job entails. If none materialises – the charity may be short-staffed and has not time to observe such niceties – you should refer to the original job ad which, hopefully, you filed away safely. You may also receive a brochure on its activities and the latest annual report.

Both documents need to be read carefully. See if you can answer the following questions:

- What is the aim of the organisation?

- Who or what does it cater for?

- What is the reach of the organisation? Is it local, regional, national, international?

- Where is the job based?

- Who are the main people in the organisation?

- Who are you likely to meet?

- Which other organisations work in the same field.

- What are the distinctive features of this one?

- What is its size: in respect to turnover, workforce?

- What do you know of its history and future plans?

Perhaps the most important piece of information you need to know is where the interview session will be held. Do you know the precise location of the building and how to get there? If you are not sure you could always phone up and ask for a map. Also you need to study your route there in order to arrive in good time. And if you are using public transport make sure you catch an earlier train or bus. There is no worse way to start an interview than to arrive late!

It is also of help if you know what form the interview will take and how long it will be so that you are not thrown off course. A large organisation may well take a full morning or even a whole day over selecting candidates and put you through a number of hurdles including:

- Psychometric tests

- Group discussion

- Panel interview

- Individual interviews.

It is therefore sensible to be prepared for everything, and if it is not evident from your invitation what form the interview will take, it does no harm to enquire beforehand. A telephone call to the person issuing the invitation is all that is needed.

Of particular importance are the questions you are likely to be asked in the interview proper. Some interviewees are thrown completely off course by a stray question that they were not expecting and start to mumble and stumble. If you have little recent experience of being interviewed, it is therefore sensible to get in some practice.

The type of questions you should be prepared for are:

- Why do you want the job?

- How much do you know about this organisation?

- In what way do your experience and qualifications equip you for this job?

- What do you feel are the main skills needed for this job?

- Where do you see yourself in five year's time?

- What are your strengths?

- What sort of qualities do you feel are needed for this job?

- What do you like to do in your spare time?

- How do you cope with pressure?

- How would you characterise yourself in a sentence?

- How good a communicator are you?

- What problems have you encountered in your working life?

- What do you most like/dislike about your current job?

- What are your salary expectations?

- What courses have you taken recently?

- What other jobs have you applied for?

- What do you consider your greatest achievement?

- What motivates you?

- How able or willing are you to make decisions?

- If offered the position, when could you start?

Some of these questions are quite tricky. With each one the selector is trying to elicit certain information about you and you need to answer them effectively. Try to turn every question into an opportunity to highlight your experience and abilities. For example:

What problems have you encountered in your working life?
I admit I've had some personal difficulties with work colleagues in the past. However, I have learned that there is no sense in harbouring grudges and the best solution is to shake hands and make up.

What motivates you?
The challenge of doing something beneficial to the community and seeing the results of my efforts. One example of this is a vacation job I had taking a group of disadvantaged youngsters on holiday to the seaside.

Practice is the key to being a successful interviewee, and if you can find someone – a friend or work colleague – who can fire the questions at you at random, you will start to cut a more convincing figure in the eyes of the interview panel. Devising model answers which you then memorise is not the way to prepare for the ordeal. You have to react spontaneously.

QUESTIONS THAT YOU SHOULD ASK THE INTERVIEWERS

Usually towards the end of the interview you will be invited to ask the interviewer or selection panel questions. While you don't have to, to avoid a long pause in the proceedings it is sensible to have a few up your sleeve. Don't, however, ask questions about matters you have already been made aware of, such as the aims of the charity in question.

- Which are your principal sources of funding?

- What are your plans for the future of the organisation?

- Is the emphasis of the charity likely to change?

- When do you hope to make an appointment?

- What opportunities are there for staff development?

- Who would I be reporting to?

- Where would I be based?

- Are there any further responsibilities attached to the post?

- How open is the organisation to new ideas?

It is best not to probe into salary and working conditions, since you don't want to appear too money conscious. Besides, you will probably have been sent such details already.

INTERVIEW DOS AND DON'TS

- Do arrive on time

- Do dress conservatively (rather than flashily or casually)

- Do maintain eye contact

- Do ask for a question to be repeated if you don't understand something

- Do be polite and courteous

- Do keep your cool

- Do try to be natural and genuine

- Do keep your answers to the point

- Don't run down your current employer

- Don't argue with the interviewer

- Don't boast

- Don't lie or exaggerate

- Don't get agitated

- Don't make jokes

- Don't talk too much

- Don't lose sight of the purpose of the interview.

AFTER THE INTERVIEW

You may hear the result of the interview immediately or you may have to wait a few days before you receive a letter. If you have landed the job, congratulations. Now you have to prove the confidence the selectors have placed in you.

If the outcome is negative, console yourself with the thought that you got this far against strong competition and have also gained useful experience of the selection process. Pick yourself up, send off some more applications and write a letter to the organisation that interviewed you thanking them for your interest in you and asking to be considered should another vacancy occur.

CHAPTER 5

The way ahead

DEVELOPING YOURSELF PROFESSIONALLY

Most people like to progress in their careers, and many voluntary organisations encourage what is known as staff development (ie they offer their employees training opportunities). Quite a few have Investors in People status, a national quality standard which indicates that they offer training of a high standard. Apart from gaining useful experience and knowledge which would be of benefit to you in any other jobs you may undertake in the future, there may well be opportunities to train for a range of professional, vocational and academic qualifications on a part-time or full-time basis.

Here is a selection of awards and courses currently available:

- Institute of Leadership and Management awards:

  ○ NVQ 3, 4 and 5 in the Management of Volunteers

- National Open College Network

  ○ Managing Voluntary & Community Organisations, levels 2 and 3 Certificate

- Managing Volunteers, level 3 Award

● Management of Volunteers, SVQ level 3 and 4

● BTEC Professional Certificate in Voluntary Sector Management (Charity Training)

● Distance learning courses from the University of Wales Lampeter:

- Certificate in Interpersonal Skills for Volunteers

- BA in Voluntary Sector Studies

● South Bank University:

- MSc/PgDip in Charity Accounting and Financial Management

- MSc/PgDip in Charity Marketing and Fundraising

- Certificate in Charity Management (ICSA)

● City University:

- MSc/PgDip in Charity Accounting and Financial Management

- MSc/PgDip in Grantmaking Management

- MSc/PgDip in Marketing and Fundraising

- MSc/PgDip in Voluntary Sector Management

● Roehampton University:

- MSc/PgDip/PgCert in Voluntary Action Management.

If you are working in fundraising The Fundraising Programme is worth considering. This is a collaboration between the Institute of Fundraising and the Directory of Social Change. It has three levels:

- Careerpoint 1: Introductory Level for those who are new to fundraising

- Careerpoint 2: Practitioner Level for practising fundraisers

- Careerpoint 3: Management Level for fundraisers who currently manage their organisations' fundraising operation.

Two of these courses lead to the Certificate of Fundraising Management awarded by the Institute of Fundraising. They are:

- **Module 1: the Foundation course in Fundraising Practice**   This is a four-day course normally conducted at the HQ of the Directory of Social Change at the end of which you are given an assignment to be completed within one year, which will be assessed by your trainer. It covers such topics as effective fundraising; how to raise money from trusts, companies and legacies; writing proposals; developing a sustainable fundraising plan; using direct mail to acquire and retain donors. Completion of this module allows Associate Members of the Institute of Fundraising to be upgraded to Full Member status.

- **Module 2: Managing Fundraising**   This course is delivered by the Projects Company. Assessment for this course is through completion of a portfolio of evidence.

The Directory of Social Change provides a wide range of other courses for the voluntary sector on such topics as marketing, communication skills, human resource management, training and development, law, health and safety regulations, volunteer management, leadership and management skills, strategy and finance.

It is also worth investigating local initiatives. For instance in the North West in 2006 there was an NVQ in Community Work Skills and Community Development Work organised by Edge Hill University of Higher Education. The course covered:

- Recruiting and supporting volunteers

- Fundraising

- Presentation skills

- Campaigning

- Equal opportunities

- Resolving conflict

- Group work.

For further information about training opportunities you should approach the Workforce Hub. This is the National Training Organisation (NTO) which serves the Voluntary Sector.

Although investing in one's future is a very sound principle, as a lowly paid charity worker you may feel you have insufficient funds to pay the fees. Moreover not every charity has sufficient surplus cash to be able to fund your studies. However, it may be possible to obtain a bursary from the Charities Aid Foundation or some other trust that offers funds to enable small and medium sized charities to grow and become more efficient. Learn Direct also offers information on grants and loans available.

CONSIDERING YOUR FUTURE

It is important to rid yourself of any notion than working in the voluntary sector is a dead end. There are drawbacks, of course, and if you are at the beginning of your career you may consider the relatively modest financial rewards a particular problem. Working for a small charity which lacks long-term, stable funding is even worse, because you feel unable to make any long-term commitments. Even key workers in the public sector (who tend to be better paid) are finding it impossible to find affordable housing in many areas in the UK.

On the other hand, if you are working for a cause you believe in you will consider that the advantages outweigh the disadvantages. You are doing work that you like and you can identify with the people (or animals) that will benefit from your efforts. People who move into the charity sector from business or government often appreciate the different working atmosphere and personal commitment that they experience.

Also remember that you are not tied down to a particular charity all your life. It is becoming quite normal for people to move around within the voluntary sector, sometimes on to better-paid jobs in larger organisations. Experience in one organisation can act as a springboard to other better established ones. You have the opportunity to expand your horizons and even pay visits abroad, particularly if you land a position in a charity operating at the international level.

Furthermore, voluntary sector staff are becoming highly regarded for their professionalism and so there is no reason why you should not try for jobs in the public sector or private enterprise. Many of skills you have acquired will be readily transferable to the worlds of business or government and, if you have backed up your work experience with professional development courses, you could find a number of useful doors will open to you.

These days the barriers between business, government and the voluntary sector are no longer as rigid as they once were. Some companies send members of their staff on secondment to charities, not only to help out the charity but also to broaden the experience of the staff themselves. And there seems no reason why people should not switch from one sector to another; even if the ethos is different, many of the skills deployed are readily transferable.

CASE STUDY 5
Martin Horwood, MP graduated in Modern History from Oxford University a began his career in a commercial organisation and then moved into the voluntary sector until he was elected to parliament.

I worked for a leading commercial advertising agency for a year working for a number of blue chip clients. But after a while I couldn't imagine spending the rest of my life selling dog food. I had got the marketing bug but I wanted to combine my marketing skills with a cause I believed in. So I joined the British Humanist Association.

Later I moved on to Help the Aged which at that time was a small charity with a staff of around one hundred. I discovered that marketing in charities has certain similarities with the commercial sector. The big difference is that direct marketing was especially important and you have a commitment to a cause.

You also have two sets of clients: the donors and the beneficiaries. The donors are less dominant than they are in commercial advertising, and the beneficiaries' voice is much stronger. This presents quite a challenge as you sometimes find yourself in conflict with your marketing instincts.

I later moved over to Oxfam to a more responsible job with a wider range of responsibilities and also because international development is one of my passions. During my time there I was posted to India to launch the Oxfam India funding scheme, which enabled me to see some of our projects at first hand: a life-changing experience.

Working with Oxfam was a great experience, but I decided I would like to go back to work for a smaller outfit and took a job as the first director of fundraising at the Alzheimer's Disease Society, now the Alzheimer's Society.

At the beginning of the new millennium my wife and I decided to move out of London when a job opportunity presented itself as a fundraising consultant with Target Direct, a company which works with a number of charities. Although this was one step removed from working within a charity I found I could engage with a number of different charities, some of them quite small.

I have since left the voluntary sector having been elected to Parliament, but continue to support and promote voluntary organisations in my new role. I feel I have had a unique career path. But to anyone thinking of following my example I would point out that the voluntary sector is just as professional as anything in the public or private sectors, and is not to be recommended to anyone who is just looking for an easy ride.

CHAPTER 6

Resources

COURSE PROVIDERS AND VALIDATORS

Centre for Charity Effectiveness
Cass Business School
City University
106 Bunhill Row
London
WC1Y 8TZ
Tel: 020 7040 8667
Website: www.city.ac.uk
Offers an MSc and Postgraduate Diploma in Voluntary Sector Management; Charity Accounting and Financial Management; Charity Marketing and Fundraising; Grantmaking Management

Charity Training
Volsector Training Centre
1 Horsegate
Deeping St James
Peterborough
PE6 8EN
Tel: 01778 344113
Website: www.charitytraining.com
Runs the BTEC Professional Certificate in Voluntary Sector Management

Department of Voluntary Sector Studies
Centre for Education and Development
University of Wales Lampeter
College Street
Lampeter
Ceredigion
SA46 7ED
Tel: 01579 424785
Website: www.volstudy.ac.uk
*Offers two distance learning courses: Certificate in Interpersonal
Skills for Volunteers; BA in Voluntary Sector Studies*

DSC Training
Directory of Social Change
24 Stephenson Way
London
NW1 2DP
Tel: 020 7391 4865
Website: www.dsc.org.uk
*Runs a number of (mainly 1–2 day) courses for the voluntary sector
on a wide range of topics including the Fundraising Programme*

Institute of Leadership and Management
Stowe House
Netherstowe
Lichfield
WS13 6TS
Tel: 01543 266867
Website: www.i-l-m.com
*Offers NVQ qualifications at levels 3, 4 and 5 in Management of
Volunteers*

National Open College Network
The Quadrant
Parkway Business Park
99 Parkway Avenue
Sheffield S9 4WG
Tel: 0114 227 0500
Website: www.nocn.org.uk
*Offers the following qualifications: Managing Voluntary &
Community Organisations, level 2 and 3 Certificate; Managing
Volunteers, level 3 Award*

Roehampton University
Erasmus House
Roehampton Lane
London
SW15 5PU
Tel: 020 8392 3232
Website: www.roehampton.ac.uk
*Offers courses at the MSc, Postgraduate Diploma and Postgraduate
Certificate levels in Voluntary Action Management*

Scottish Qualifications Authority
Hanover House
24 Douglas Street
Glasgow
G2 7NQ
Tel: 08452 791000
Website: www.sqa.org.uk
Awards SVQs in Management of Volunteers, levels 3 and 4

South Bank University
103 Borough Road
London
SE1 0AA
Website: www.lsbu.ac.uk
Email: bcim@lsbu.ac.uk
*Offers MSc and Postgraduate Diploma courses in Charity
Accounting and Financial Management; Charity Marketing and
Fundraising. It also runs a course leading to the Certificate in
Charity Management, which it has developed in association with the
Institute of Chartered Secretaries and Administrators (ICSA)*

Working for a Charity
National Council for Voluntary Organisations
Regents Wharf
8 All Saints' Street
London N1 9RL
Tel: 020 7520 2512
Website: www.working foracharity.org.uk
*Introductory training programmes to working in the voluntary
sector*

RECRUITMENT AGENCIES AND WEBSITES

Aquilas
46 Culver Road
St Albans
AL1 4ED
Tel: 01727 375361
Website: www.aquilas.co.uk

CF Appointments
Lloyds Court
1 Goodman's Yard
London
E1 8AT
Tel: 020 7953 1190
Website: www.cfappointments.com

Charity Action Recruitment
5–13 Trinity Street
London
SE1 1DB
Tel: 020 7378 5441/5442
Website: www.c-a-r.org.uk

Charity Careers
1 Chertsey Road
Woking
GU21 5AB
Tel: 08700 131200
Website: www.charitycareers.co.uk

Charity Connections
15 Seed Street
Waterloo
London
SE1 8ST
Tel: 020 7202 9000
Website: www.charityconnections.co.uk

Charity Futures
35 Plymouth Road
Penarth
Cardiff
CF64 3DA
Tel: 029 2070 6999
Website: www.charityfutures.com

Charity Job
Jobladder Ltd
PO Box 762A
Surbiton
KT5 8YZ
Website: www.charityjob.co.uk

Charity People
Palladia Central Court
25 Southampton Buildings
London
WC2A 1AL
Tel: 08451 284341
Website: www.charitypeople.com

Charity Recruitment
40 Rosebery Avenue
London
EC1R 4RN
Tel: 020 7833 0770
Website: www.charityopps.com

Eden Brown
17–29 Sun Street
London
EC2M 2PS
Tel: 020 7309 1300
Website: www.edenbrown.co.uk

Execucare
34 Ebury Street
London
SW1W 0LU
Tel: 020 7761 0700
Website: www.execucare.com

Flow Caritas
Unit 2
38 Copperfield Street
London
SE1 0EA
Tel: 020 7939 9973
Website: www.flowcaritas.co.uk.

Harris Hill
The Atrium Suite
Bishops Palace House
Riverside Walk
Kingston on Thames
KT1 1QN
Tel: 020 8974 9990
Website: www.harrishill.co.uk

Jobs in Charities
63A The Avenue
Wraysbury
TW19 5EY
Tel: 08701 417029
Website: www.jobsincharities.co.uk

Kage Partnership
Linton House
164–180 Union Street
London
SE1 0LH
Tel: 020 7926 3434
Website: www.kagep.com

Lifeline Personnel
122 Great Portland Street
London
W1W 6LN
Tel: 020 7637 3737
Website: www.lifeline-personnel.com

Oxford Human Resource Consultants
Oxford Centre for Innovation
Mill Street
Oxford
OX2 0JX
Tel: 01865 201515
Website: www.oxfordhr.co.uk
Recruits for overseas development agencies

NfP Resourcing (Sycal Group)
6 Northernhay Place
Exeter
Devon
EX4 3QJ
Tel: 01392 254978
Website: www.nfp-resourcing.org.uk

ProspectUs
20–22 Stukeley Street
London
WC2B 5LR
Tel: 020 7691 1925
Website: www.prospect-us.co.uk

The Principle Partnership
52 Lime Street
London
EC2M 7AF
Tel: 020 7198 6000
Website: www.tpp.co.uk

CHARITY RECRUITMENT FAIR ORGANISERS

Charity Fair
Directory of Social Change
24 Stephenson Way
London
NW1 2DP
Tel: 020 7391 4800
Website: www.dsc.org.uk
This fair takes place in September/October in London, Manchester and Oxford

Forum 3
Charity People
Palladia Central Court
25 Southampton Buildings
London
WC2A 1AL
Website: www.forum3.co.uk
The Forum 3 Fair usually takes place in the autumn

Society Guardian Live Jobs Fair
119 Farringdon Road
London
EC1R 3ER
Tel: 020 7278 2332
Website: www.guardian.co.uk/jobs

SOURCES OF INFORMATION

Association of Chief Executives of Voluntary Organisations (ACEVO)
1 New Oxford Street
London
WC1A 1NU
Tel: 08453 458481
Website: www.acevo.org.uk

Association of Medical Research Charities
61 Grays Inn Road
London
WC1X 8TL
Tel: 020 7269 8820
Website: www.amrc.org.uk

Charities Aid Foundation (CAF)
25 King's Hill Avenue
King's Hill
West Malling
Kent
ME19 4TA
Tel: 01732 520000
Website: www.caf.org.uk

Charity Commission for England and Wales
PO Box 1155
Liverpool
L69 3XR
Website: www.charity-commission.gov.uk

Directory of Social Change
24 Stephenson Way
London
NW1 2DP
Tel: 020 7391 4800
Website: www.dsc.org.uk

Family Welfare Association
501–505 Kingsland Road
London
E8 4AU
Tel: 020 7245 6251
Website: www.fwa.org.uk

Guidestar UK
17 Exeter Street
London
WC2E 7DU
Tel: 020 7240 1969
Website: www.guidestar.org.uk

Institute of Fundraising
Market Towers
5th Floor
1 Nine Elms Lane
London
SW8 5NQ
Tel: 020 7626 3436

National Council for Voluntary Organisations
Regents Wharf
8 All Saints' Street
London
N1 9RL
Tel: 020 7713 6161
Website: www.ncvo-vol.org.uk

Northern Ireland Council for Voluntary Action
61 Duncairn Gardens
Belfast
BT15 2GB
Tel: 028 9087 7777
Website: www.nicva.org

Scottish Council for Voluntary Organisations (SCVO)
Mansfield Traquair Centre
15 Mansfield Place
Edinburgh
EH3 6BB
Tel: 0131 556 3882
Website: www.scvo.org.uk

Wales Council for Voluntary Action
Baltic House
Mount Stuart Square
Cardiff Bay
Cardiff
CF19 5FH
Tel: 08706 071666
Website: www.wcva.org.uk

ADDRESSES OF SELECTED VOLUNTARY ORGANISATIONS MENTIONED IN THIS BOOK

Please note that the inclusion of an organisation in this list does not denote that it is currently recruiting staff or has any vacancies. You should check with their website for the availability of jobs on offer before you contact any of them.

Age Concern England
Bramah House
65–71 Bermondsey Street
London
SE1 3XF
Tel: 0800 009966
Website: www.ageconcern.org.uk

Alzheimer's Society
Gordon House
10 Greencoat House
Greencoat Place
London
SW1P 1PH
Tel: 020 7306 0606
Website: www.alzheimers.org.uk

Amnesty International
99–119 Rosebery Avenue
London
EC1R 4RE
Tel: 020 7814 6200
Website: www.amnesty.org.uk

Barnardo's
Tanner's Lane
Barkingside
Ilford
Essex
IG6 1QG
Tel: 020 8550 8822
Website: www.barnardos.org.uk

Blue Cross
Shilton Road
Burford
Oxfordshire
OX18 4PF
Tel: 01993 822657
Website: www.bluecross.org.uk

British Executive Service Overseas (BESO)
164 Vauxhall Bridge Road
London
SW1V 2RB
Tel: 020 7630 0644
Website: www.beso.org

British Heart Foundation
14 Fitzhardinge Street
London
W1H 6DH
Tel: 020 7935 0185
Website: www.bhf.org.uk

British Red Cross
Moorfields House
Moorfields
London
EC2Y 9AL
Tel: 020 7235 5454
Website: www.redcross.org.uk

Bully Free Zone
23 Palace Street
Bolton
BL1 2DR
Website: www.bullyfreezone.co.uk

BUNAC
16 Bowling Green Lane
London
EC1 0QH
Tel: 020 7251 3472
Website: www.bunac.org.uk

Campaign Against Drinking and Driving
PO Box 62
Brighouse
West Yorkshire
HD6 3YY
Tel: 08451 235541/235543
Website: www.cadd.org.uk

Campaign for Nuclear Disarmament
162 Holloway Road
London
N7 8DQ
Tel: 020 7700 2393
Website: www.cnd.uk.org

Cancer Research UK
61 Lincoln's Inn Fields
London
WC2A 3PX
Tel: 020 7061 8400
Website: www.cancerresearchuk.org

Carers UK
20–25 Glasshouse Yard
London
EC1A 4JT
Tel: 020 7490 8818
Website: www.carersuk.org

Childline
45 Folgate Street
London
E1 6GL
Tel: 020 7650 3200
Website: www.childline.org.uk

Children's Society
Edward Rudolf House
Margey Street
London WC1X 0JL
Tel: 020 7841 4400
Website: www.childrenssociety.org.uk

Community Service Volunteers (CSV)
237 Pentonville Road
London
N1 9NJ
Tel: 020 7278 6601
Website: www.csv.org.uk

Cruse Bereavement Care
Cruse House
116 Sheen Road
Richmond
Surrey
TW9 1UR
Tel: 08701 671677
Website: www.cruse.org.uk

Earthwatch
367 Banbury Road
Oxford
OX2 7HT
Tel: 01865 318838
Website: www.earthwatch.org/europe

Friends of the Earth
27–28 Underwood Street
London
N1 7JQ
Tel: 020 7490 1555
Website: www.foe.co.uk

Frontier
50–52 Rivington Street
London
EC2A 3QP
Tel: 020 7613 2422
Website: www.frontierprojects.ac.uk

GAP Challenge
Black Arrow House
2 Chandos Road
London
NW10 6NF
Tel: 020 8728 7200
Website: www.gap-challenge.co.uk

Greenpeace
Canonbury Villas
London
N1 2PN
Tel: 020 7865 8100
Website: www.greenpeace.org

Help the Aged
207–221 Pentonville Road
London
N1 9UZ
Tel: 020 7278 1114
Website: www.helptheaged.org.uk

Hospice Information Service
St Christopher's Hospice
51–59 Lawrie Park Road
Sydenham
London
SE26 6DZ
Tel: 08709 033903
Website: www.hospiceinformation.info

Howard League for Penal Reform
1 Ardleigh Road
London
N1 4HS
Tel: 020 7249 7373
Website: www.howardleague.org

i to i
Woodside House
261 Low Lane
Leeds
LS18 5NY
Tel: 0113 205 4620
Website: www.i-to-i.com

IFAW (International Fund for Animal Welfare)
Camelford House
87–90 Albert Embankment
London
SE1 9UD
Tel: 020 7587 7600
Website: www.ifaw.org

International Refugee Trust
PO Box 31452
Chiswick
London
W4 4JG
Tel: 020 8994 9120
Website: www.irt.org.uk

Leonard Cheshire
30 Millbank
London
SW1 4QD
Tel: 020 7802 8200
Website: www.leonard-cheshire.org

Macmillan Cancer Relief
89 Albert Embankment
London
SE1 7UQ
Tel: 020 7840 7840
Website: www.macmillan.org.uk

Mentoring and Befriending Foundation
First Floor
Charles House

Albert Street
Eccles
Manchester
M30 0PW
Tel: 0161 787 8600
Website: www.mandbf.org.uk

MERLIN (Medical Emergency Relief International)
56–64 Leonard Street
London
EC2A 4LT
Tel: 020 7065 0800
Website: www.merlin.org.uk

Mind
Granta House
15–19 Broadway
London
E15 4BQ
Tel: 020 8519 2122
Website: www.mind.org.uk

NACRO (National Association for the Care and Rehabilitation of Offenders)
169 Clapham Road
London
SW9 0PU
Tel: 020 7582 6500
Website: www.nacro.org.uk

National Federation of Citizens' Advice Bureaux
115–123 Pentonville Road
London N1 9LZ
Tel: 020 7833 2181
Website: www.citizensadvice.org,uk

National Trust
Rowan House
Kembrey Park
Swindon
SN2 6UG
Tel: 01793 462800
Website: www.nationaltrust.org.uk

NCH
65 Highbury Park
London
N5 1UD
Tel: 020 7704 7000
Website: www.nch.org.uk

NSPCC
Weston House
42 Curtain Road
London
EC2A 3NH
Tel: 020 8625 2500
Website: www.nspcc.org.uk

Oxfam
Oxfam House
John Smith Drive
Oxford
OX4 2JY
Tel: 08702 222700
Website: www.oxfam.org.uk

PDSA
Whitechapel Way
Priorslee
Telford
TF2 9PQ
Tel: 01952 290999
Website: www.pdsa.org.uk

Prince's Trust
18 Park Square East
London
NW1 4LH
Tel: 020 7543 1234
Website: www.princes-trust.org.uk

Quest Overseas
32 Clapham Mansions
Nightingale Lane
London
SW4 9AQ
Tel: 020 8673 8585
Website: www.questoverseas.com

Raleigh International
Raleigh House
27 Parsons Green Lane
London
SW6 4HZ
Tel: 020 7371 8585
Website: www.raleighinternational.org.uk

Rare Breeds Survival Trust
National Agricultural Centre
Stoneleigh Park
Kenilworth
CV8 2LG
Tel: 02476 696551
Website: www.rbst.org.uk

Refugee Council
240–250 Ferndale Road
London
SW9 8DB
Tel: 020 7346 6700
Website: www.refugeecouncil.org.uk

RNLI
West Quay Road
Poole
BH15 1HZ
Tel: 08451 226999
Website: ww.rnli.org.uk

Royal British Legion
408 Pall Mall
London
SW1Y 5JY
Tel: 020 7973 7200
Website: www.britishlegion.org.uk

Royal MENCAP Society
123 Golden Lane
London
EC1Y 0RT
Tel: 020 7454 0454
Website: www.mencap.org.uk

Royal National Institute for the Blind
105 Judd Street
London
WC1H 9NE
Tel: 020 7388 1266
Website: www.rnib.org.uk

Royal National Institute for the Deaf
19–25 Featherstone Street
London
EC1Y 8SL
Tel: 020 7296 8000
Website: www.rnid.org.uk

RSPB
The Lodge
Sandy
Bedfordshire
SG19 2DL
Tel: 01767 680551
Website: www.rspb.org.uk

RSPCA
Wilberforce Way
Southwater
Horsham
West Sussex
RH13 9RS
Tel: 08700 101181
Website: www.rspca.org.uk

Save the Children
St John's Lane
London
EC1M 4AR
Tel: 020 7012 6400
Website: www.savethechildren.org.uk

Scope
PO Box 833
Milton Keynes
MK12 5NY
Tel: 08088 003333
Website: www.scope.org.uk

Shelter
88 Old Street
London
EC1V 9HU
Tel: 020 7505 2000
Website: www.shelter.org.uk

St John Ambulance
27 St John's Lane
London
EC1M 4BU
Tel: 08700 104950
Website: www.sja.org.uk

Teaching and Projects Abroad
Gerrard House
Rustington
West Sussex
BN16 1AW
Tel: 01903 859911
Website: www.teaching-abroad.co.uk

Travellers
7 Mulberry Close
Ferring
West Sussex
BN12 5HY
Tel: 01903 502595
Website: www.travellersworldwide.com

Voluntary Service Overseas (VSO)
317 Putney Bridge Road
London
SW15 2PN
Tel: 020 8780 7200
Website: www.vso.org.uk

Wildfowl and Wetland Trust
Slimbridge
Gloucestershire
GL2 7BT
Tel: 01453 891900
Website: www.wwt.org.uk

WWF
Panda House
Weyadie Park
Godalming
Surrey
GU7 1XR
Tel: 01483 426444
Website: www.wwf.org.uk

YMCA
640 Forest Road
London
E17 3DZ
Tel: 020 8520 5599
Website: www.ymca.org.uk

USEFUL PUBLICATIONS

MAGAZINES AND NEWSPAPERS
Fundraising
17 Errington Road
Colchester
CO3 3EA
Tel: 01206 579081
Website: www.fundraising.co.uk
An online magazine

Guardian
119 Farringdon Road
London
EC1R 3ER
Website: www.guardian.co.uk
Monday, Tuesday, Wednesday and Saturday editions

NFP Jobs
Conference House Ltd
Silver Ley
Farley Green
Stradishall
Newmarket
CB8 8OY
Tel: 08797 367367
Website: http://nfpjobs.netxtra.net
An online jobs newsletter

Professional Fundraising
Plaza Publishing
3 Rectory Grove
London
SW4 0DX
Tel: 020 7819 1200
Website: www.professionalfundraising.co.uk

Social Caring, Care and Health
Golden Cross House
4th Floor
Duncannon Street
Strand
London
WC2N 4JF
Tel: 08709 017773
Website: www.careandhealth.com

Third Sector
Haymarket Publications
174 Hammersmith Road
London
W8 7JP
Tel: 020 8267 5000

VS Magazine
NCVO
Regents Wharf
All Saints Street
London
N1 9RL
Website: www.vsmagazine.org

HANDBOOKS AND DIRECTORIES
Charity Choice: The Encyclopaedia of Charities (Waterlow
Professional Publishing, 2005)
*Provides information on over 8000 charities. Also publishes as
separate volumes:* Charity Choice Scotland, Charity Choice Northern
Ireland

Charity Trends (Caritas Data)
Provides analysis of the performance of the top 500 fundraising charities

The Major Charities: An Independent Guide, Luke Herbert and Kathryn Becker (Directory for Social Change, 2002)
Contains detailed entries on 165 major charities, 30 group entries (eg on hospices and cancer care charities) and a list of the top 500 fundraising charities

The Top 100 Charities in Scotland (Caritas Data).

The Voluntary Sector Almanac: The State of the Sector (NCVO, 2006)

Voluntary Agencies Directory (NCVO, 2006)
Lists 2000 voluntary and charitable organisations with details of their aims, objectives, financial matters and contact details

Who's Who in Charities (Caritas Data)
Biographies of people working for the UK's top charities

Working in the Voluntary Sector, Craig Brown (How To Books, 2005)